BEACON HILL

In memory of
Roger Allan Moore
1931 – 1990
"The conscience of Beacon Hill"

BEACON HILL

A LIVING PORTRAIT

Barbara W. Moore and Gail Weesner

PHOTOGRAPHS BY SOUTHIE BURGIN

ILLUSTRATIONS BY CONSTANCE SCHNITGER

CENTRY HILL PRESS
Boston, Massachusetts

DESIGNER: *Dede Cummings*
COPY EDITOR: *Anne Swanson*
PRINTER: *South China Printing Company Limited, Hong Kong*

Endpapers: The scene on the endpapers presents "A Prospective *[sic]* View of Part of the Common," a 1768 watercolor by Christian Remick. This view records the south slope of Beacon Hill as it appeared in the decades just prior to development. The landmarks seen in this view are, from left to right: three frame houses that were soon to be acquired by artist John Singleton Copley; the rooftop of the country residence of lawyer Humphrey Davie; the Thomas Hancock estate; and the beacon.

Published in 1992 by Centry Hill Press, Box 306, Charles Street Station, Boston, Massachusetts 02114

Library of Congress Catalog Card Number 91-78259

ISBN 0-9632077-0-9 (cloth)
ISBN 0-9632077-1-7 (paper)

INTRODUCTION

IN RECENT YEARS the name of our neighborhood has been assigned to a TV mini-series, a line of bed linens, and a very rich chocolate chip cookie. From the trolley-car tours that ply the boundaries of the Beacon Hill Historic District, we overhear the prepared banter — a compendium of all the myths and inaccuracies so frequently associated with Beacon Hill, none of which has much to do with the place we live or the people who live here.

Thomas Bailey Aldrich, a New Hampshire native who resided successively on Charles, Pinckney, and Mount Vernon streets, once declared that "Though I am not genuine-Boston, I am Boston-plated." In like manner, we can claim to be Beacon Hill-plated. Together, we combine more than fifty years of Beacon Hill living.

We both came to Boston as newly-marrieds. At a time when both members of a couple worked, the Hill seemed to be a good place to live. It provided urbanity, a pleasant ambiance, and a convenient location for husbands who both worked late. We never thought that we were choosing a permanent home.

As the years passed, we settled into houses and raised children. We experienced the many exasperations and challenges of urban family living, and we saw many friends leave for an easier life in the suburbs — especially in the late 1960s and early 1970s, when drugs and even violence spilled into the neighborhood. But like many of our neighbors, we persisted. The neighborhood "improved" and the property values (and taxes) began to rise. Today our houses are (almost) renovated; our streets are (usually) picturesque and serene; and along with our neighbors we (generally) consider ourselves lucky to be here. Nevertheless, we have spent most of these years answering the well-meant question, "Why do you live in such a place?" We hope the answer is contained in this book.

Beacon Hill is a lively community of approximately 10,000 residents with varied interests, social and economic backgrounds, and talents. Perhaps because we have shared common challenges, we are an unusually stable and close-knit community, but one that offers privacy as well. We live within walking distance of most urban amenities and services. Moreover, the everyday world about us is a source of never-ending interest and pleasure.

When we began thinking about this book, we were confident that we knew Beacon Hill well. More than a year later, we are humbled. The history and the fabric of this small place are unbelievably rich and engrossing. It is with great reluctance that we have limited this book to its present scope. We trust it presents an honest portrait.

NOTE:

Assigning a precise date for almost any nineteenth-century building on Beacon Hill is a dangerous business. In preparing this book we were faced with a choice: (1) to avoid using many dates at all — which though it might please some, would be unacceptable to others, including ourselves; (2) to discuss or qualify each date that was questionable — which would expand the scope of this book and be tedious for most readers; (3) to undertake independent research of any questionable date — which would be prohibitively time-consuming and probably often fruitless; or (4) to plunge forward, with the hope that our readers will understand that we have done our best. In general, our rule has been to abide by certain respected sources, such as Allen Chamberlain's *Beacon Hill: Its Ancient Pastures and Early Mansions* (1924) or A. McVoy McIntyre's *Beacon Hill: A Walking Tour* (1975). In the case of Bulfinch buildings, we have relied on Harold Kirker's 1969 *The Architecture of Charles Bulfinch*. If work on a particular building extended over several years, we either indicate this circumstance or use the date of completion.

Secondly, our short lists of Noted Residents for the various Beacon Hill streets is admittedly rather frivolous, because they are not complete and may even be misleading. In an era of boarding houses and seasonal rentals, some of Beacon Hill's most noted residents lived rather transiently: Louisa May Alcott, for example, lived in at least six locations, and we have traced Julia Ward Howe to about as many Beacon Hill addresses.

In both these matters, we welcome any corrections or comments, and we pledge to maintain a file of such responses so they can be included in any future editions of this book.

CONTENTS

TRIMOUNTAIN REMEMBERED
A Short History of Beacon Hill

Against the modern Boston skyline, Beacon Hill casts a modest silhouette — a gentle rising of red brick, defined primarily by the golden State House dome. This familiar view gives little hint of the hill's original dimensions. It was once considerably higher and more massive, called a mountain and mentioned by almost every early visitor to the town. The first published description of Boston (1634), by an English traveler named William Wood, tells of "a high Mountaine with three little Hills rising on top of it, wherefore it is called the Tramount." The Tramount (also Traemont, Tremont, or Trimountain) was to generations of Bostonians the most prominent topographical feature of their town. Later, it became the focus of a remarkably successful real estate development, which transformed the rugged slopes into a fashionable residential district and sculpted the hill to its present size and shape.

THE PENINSULA

The site of the early settlement was a barren, wind-blown peninsula, about a mile wide, less than three miles long, and joined to the mainland by a narrow neck (Figure 1). It must have resembled hundreds of other points of land that jut into the Atlantic along the northern New England coast, with rocky cliffs and sandy beaches, coves and inlets, tidal pools and salt marshes. And rising above it all was the geologic backbone of the peninsula, the three-peaked glacial ridge known as Trimountain.

Perhaps because it was windswept, or perhaps because of earlier clearing by Indians, the peninsula was sparsely wooded, covered with grass and scrub growth but with few large trees. Anne Pollard, who arrived as a young girl in the first boatload of settlers and who lived to be, at 105, the oldest citizen of Boston, recalled toward the end of her life the terrain she knew as a child: "very uneven, abounding in small hollows and swamps, and covered with blueberry and other bushes."

By all accounts, the Trimountain was similarly barren — rough and rocky, and overgrown with brushwood and brambles. Springs and small brooks tumbled down the hillslopes. A nineteenth-century

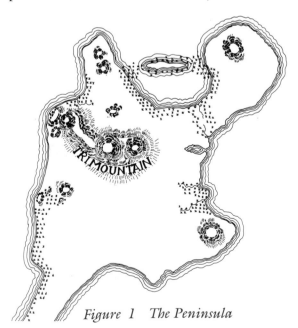

Figure 1   The Peninsula

drawing (Figure 2) shows the hill's distinctive profile: a ridge or range of hills running through the center of the peninsula, dominated by a cone-shaped central peak and flanked by smaller risings to the east and to the west.

Figure 2   Trimountain from Charlestown

THE REVEREND MR. BLAXTON

The peninsula had an Indian name — Shawmut — but no Indians lived there when the first permanent settlers arrived. Rather, the entire point was claimed by an eccentric Church of England clergyman, William Blaxton (or Blackstone). A shadowy figure, Blaxton had come to Massachusetts Bay in 1623, doing brief missionary service in Weymouth and then establishing himself on Shawmut peninsula, where by 1627 he was living on the southwestern slope of the Trimountain, in a comfortable cottage with a rose garden nearby. By most accounts this was somewhere on the slope overlooking Boston Common, most probably in the vicinity of Spruce Street. (See Beacon Hill map, page 24.) It is also known that he owned an excellent spring (thought by many to be in the vicinity of Louisburg Square) and that he planted a fine orchard (some say near the junction of Pinckney and West Cedar streets). Moreover, Blaxton reputedly possessed a library of 200 volumes, prompting Van Wyck Brooks to quip that "there have been books on the slope of Beacon Hill when the wolves still howled on the summit."

THE PURITANS

In June of 1630 a band of roughly one thousand English men, women, and children sailed into Boston Harbor, the first wave of a great movement of Puritans fleeing the England of Charles I. They joined a small English settlement in Charlestown, across the Charles River estuary from Shawmut, but they soon found that the site lacked an adequate supply of fresh water. Then, for reasons we will never know, the reclusive Blaxton invited the entire company to his side of the river, where, he advised them, there was a very good spring from which flowed excellent water. (Indeed, it is said that the word Shawmut meant "fountains of living water.") Accepting Blaxton's proposal, the Puritans moved their settlement to the peninsula across the bay, which they promptly renamed Boston after the town in East Anglia from which many of them had come.

While the new town hugged the harbor, Blaxton remained at a safe distance on his hillside. Apparently he came to regret his generosity, and some four years later he announced he was leaving the place. Selling all his Shawmut land except a six-acre plot surrounding his cottage, he left Boston for Rhode Island, where his death was recorded in 1675.

THE EARLY YEARS

Tradition quotes Blaxton that he "had left England because of his dislike of the Lord Bishops, and now he did not like the Lord Brethren." If so, he had good cause to flee Massachusetts Bay. A flood tide of Puritan immigration was underway, and between 1630 and 1640, twenty thousand of the Lord Brethren would sail into Boston Harbor. Many passed through the port, moving on to establish the farms and villages that soon dotted the Massachusetts countryside, but others stayed in Boston, whose population had swelled to almost 4000 by the year of Blaxton's departure. Thereafter the town grew more slowly, reaching 7000 by the end of the decade and 16,000 on the eve of the Revolution. The young town first expanded along the shores of the peninsula, then crept slowly inland, its character evolving from provincial outpost to thriving port.

TRIMOUNTAIN

As the town grew, Trimountain languished. Only its lower slopes were hospitable, and for more than a century it remained a lonely, looming place, used mostly as pastureland with a scattering of small orchards here and there. From an early date its spurs served the town as gravel pits, and by 1730 some of its slopes had been appropriated for ropemaking. This was a smelly business, highly combustible, and requiring large open stretches of land for the "walks," the long, narrow wooden buildings in which the ropes were made.

The hill's three summits had separate names and identities, and each peak had a somewhat different history. The map (Figure 3) shows the Trimount's original topography superimposed on a modern street plan. The eastern hill, now an undistinguished

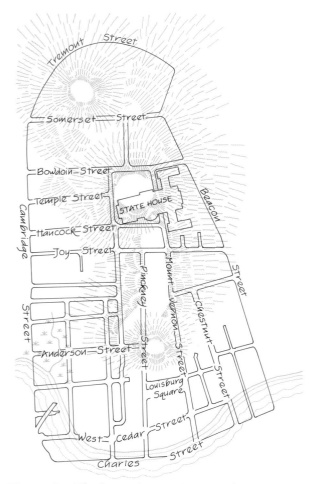

Figure 3   The Summits of Trimountain

quarter of mixed governmental and commercial buildings, was once a place of great beauty. It was first called Cotton Hill after the Reverend John Cotton, who lived on its flank. Because its slope was gentle and oriented toward the harbor, it was the first part of the Trimountain to be populated. It became the site of suburban estates, including that of merchant Peter

Faneuil. In 1835 these gracious old places were demolished and the hill, by then renamed Pemberton Hill, was reduced by some 60 feet to make way for a real estate development centered around a fashionable residential square. Pemberton Square (see page 113) was in its day much admired for its elegance and beauty, but sadly it was razed — the western half in the 1880s and the opposite side in the early 1960s to make way for the ambitious Government Center redevelopment project.

West of Cotton Hill rose the central summit of the Trimountain, the dominant cone-shaped peak. Its highest point, located just west of the new State House park, commanded a panoramic view of the harbor and surrounding countryside. Perhaps because its heights were used as a lookout, or perhaps because of its central position, the early settlers called it Centry Hill. Before long, however, it acquired the name of Beacon Hill.

THE BEACON

In 1634 — the same year that William Blaxton left Boston — the ruling General Court proclaimed that "there shalbe forthwith a beacon sett on the centry hill at Boston, to give notice to the country of any danger." Accordingly, there soon rose upon this highest point in town the rather primitive structure that gave the hill its modern name.

The beacon stood for a century and a half; again and again, it appears in early maps and views, itself a lofty sentry. Certainly repaired and probably rebuilt from time to time (which may explain why even eyewitness descriptions differ), it was most often characterized as a tall pole or mast (Figure 4), at the top of which was mounted an iron pot filled with combustibles. Supported by triangular braces, it was fitted with rungs for climbing the pole in order to ignite a beacon fire.

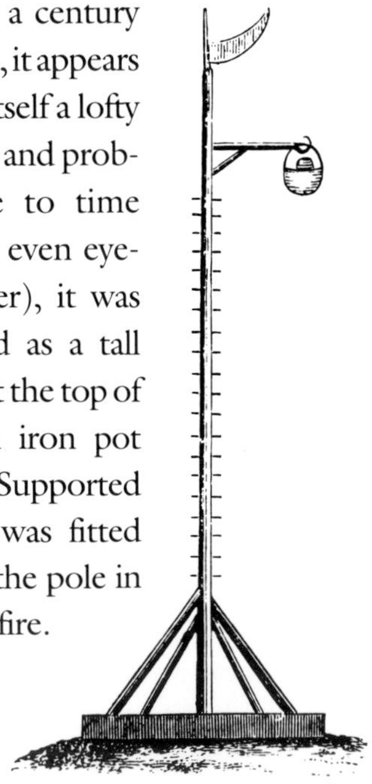

Figure 4   The Beacon

Rising 60 feet above the hill's summit (which was itself about 65 feet higher than today), a blazing beacon would have been visible from a great distance. There is, however, no record that the pot was ever fired. The Puritans enjoyed good relations with the local Indians, and until the events leading to the Revolution, Boston was a peaceful town. The beacon site became a popular place, renowned for its view. It occupied a parcel of town land that was described as a grassy hemisphere with a flat top "six rods square" — 99 feet on each side. A lane named Sentry Street led from the Common to the beacon, which was only attained by a strenuous climb, with the aid of toe holds worn in the slope.

South of the beacon mound the hill dropped gently toward the Common. Around 1700, this sunny slope started attracting residents, and by midcentury several substantial structures stood along a new street named Beacon.

THE HANCOCK HOUSE

The most famous of these properties and the one that survived longest was the great stone mansion built in 1737 by the merchant Thomas Hancock (Figure 5). Reckoned among the finest houses in Boston, it was inherited in 1777 by Thomas's nephew John, the rich young revolutionary who later became the first governor of the independent colony of Massachusetts. This property, with some six acres of gardens and pasture, was destined to become prime real estate. The house survived until 1863, when it was demolished amid cries of protest.

Beyond the Hancock estate, Beacon Street trailed on toward the Back Bay shores, skirting the base of the third hill of the Trimount. This western peak, the most remote, was extremely rough and steep, and for much of its history it even lacked a proper name. The slope facing the water, originally Blaxton's property, was once called West Hill. Then, beginning in 1769, much of this hillside was acquired by the artist John Singleton Copley. When Copley left for Europe four years later, he owned three wooden houses and about 18 acres — a sizable property on a small peninsula — and thus the vicinity of his estate was sometimes known as Copley's Hill.

Figure 5   The Hancock House

This westernmost peak stood just east of today's Louisburg Square, from where it dropped sharply toward the river, terminating in a high cliff overlooking the Cambridge shore. Harrison Gray Otis, one of the men most responsible for its transformation, would recall years later that Mount Vernon (its patriotic new name) was once "very rough and mountainous and rarely visited by anybody." According to another reminiscence given the same year by an elderly citizen named Joseph Montcrief, the area in his youth was "exactly like the country." By most accounts its summit was almost as high as Beacon Hill.

MOUNT WHOREDOM

Compared with the pleasant rural atmosphere of the new Beacon Street estates, the northern slope of "Copley's Hill" was, in effect, another world. From an early date it was the site of a small, isolated community called West Boston. By around 1730, maps indicate a tidy grid of streets nestled behind the Trimountain. Anchored by Cambridge Street, the settlement moved up the northern flank as far as present Revere Street, with some of the streets, such as Garden and Grove, bearing their modern names.

The district began as a waterfront community and soon developed a rough-and-tumble character. During the British occupation it was apparently frequented by soldiers, and it was about this time — and on English military maps — that one encounters the name Mount Whoredom.

This area kept its bawdy reputation well into the next century. Here, it was reported, "whole nights are spent in drinking and carousing. . . ." Here "it is confidently affirmed and fully believed, there are three hundred females wholly devoid of shame and modesty." In 1823 the area was forcibly cleaned up under the personal leadership of Mayor Josiah Quincy, and in the decades that followed it moved toward middle-class respectability, with trim brick row houses interspersed with the freestanding wooden structures that had typified the earlier settlement. At the end of the century the neighborhood again changed character, becoming an immigrant quarter, with tall brick tenements to house the newcomers from South and Central Europe.

Thus, today's North Slope was a separate development from its earliest years — a distinction that persists to the present day, evidenced in its architectural diversity and in an almost separate street pattern (only Joy and West Cedar streets connect the two sides of the hill).

BRITISH OCCUPATION

For the people of Boston, the most eventful times in the struggle for independence were the eight years before the Declaration was signed. From September 1768 to March 1776, while British troops occupied their town, Bostonians witnessed a series of legendary clashes between local Patriots and English authority: the Boston Massacre, the Tea Party, the battles at Lexington and Concord and Bunker Hill, and then finally, Washington's triumphant occupation of Dorchester Heights.

As these events unfolded the Trimount assumed military importance. It was a natural lookout and largely uninhabited. As tensions grew these heights were fortified, and British barracks were built against the hillsides. Redoubts were constructed on the southern and western slopes, and an open breastwork was thrown up near the foot of Pinckney Street.

From these years come a number of interesting vignettes: a foiled attempt by Patriots to light the beacon fire; a mixed crowd of Tories, Patriots, and British soldiers gathered near the beacon to witness the battle raging in Charlestown; a mortar battery near today's Louisburg Square shelling the rebels in Cambridge as "boys and other idlers, even women, stood by the gunners to mark the shots." Then, finally, the town's beacon was torn down by order of the British General Thomas Gage and the proud Hancock mansion occupied as headquarters for General Sir Henry Clinton.

A valuable by-product of these years was a proliferation of military maps and views, prepared not only

Figure 6   View from Beacon Hill

by the British but also by the French, who were keenly interested in England's colonial troubles. Among these documents are a series of several watercolors comprising a panoramic view from the summit of Beacon Hill, prepared by "Lt. Williams of the R. W. Fuzeliers." The view to the west, seen opposite (Figure 6), presents a picture of the Trimountain ridge from a location just behind the State House park (Beacon Hill) to a point just above Louisburg Square (keyed number 18 and identified as "Mount Whoredam"). The long, low structures to the right of the western hill may be the ropewalks that stood between Pinckney and Myrtle streets; to the north, just visible against the water line, are the rooftops of the disreputable community of West Boston. The tents in the left foreground probably housed British troops; across the river rises the town of Cambridge.

THE MONUMENT

When the British troops evacuated in March 1776, Boston again became a civilian town. The beacon was re-erected in the center of a small fort that had been built in its place. It stood until 1789, when it blew down in a November storm. Shortly thereafter came a proposal that the beacon be replaced with an entirely different kind of structure — a memorial column to commemorate the events of the recent War for Independence.

This scheme was conceived, promoted, and executed by a young man whose name would be closely linked with that of Beacon Hill. Charles Bulfinch, a 26-year-old Harvard graduate, had recently returned from a grand tour of Europe, where he had greatly admired the classical style, both new and antique. By subscription, he gathered the funds necessary to erect a Doric column on the mound where the beacon had stood. The shaft, some 60 feet high, was surmounted by a wooden eagle, gilded and "set up to serve as a weather vane." Attached to the base were four plaques commemorating events of the recent war.

This new adornment was generally admired, and the summit of Beacon Hill became even more popular as a place of resort. Bostonians offered extravagant testimonials to the grandeur of Beacon Hill and the beauty of the view from its heights. A 1792 visitor to the site records: "Took a stroll on Beacon Hill, from the summit whereof one may behold the most variegated and luxuriant scenery. . . . Our friends did not fail to express their admiration of the delightful prospect, and to declare that neither in Europe nor in any other part of America, did they ever enjoy so charming a view."

This view would soon disappear. The six rods square of town land was surrounded by private property that was becoming increasingly valuable. Even before embarking on his monument project, Charles Bulfinch had submitted to Massachusetts authorities plans for a new State House, to be built at an undetermined location. After seven years' consideration, the bureaucrats of the day approved the plans and a site was purchased: The new State House was to rise from the Beacon Hill pasture of the late Governor Hancock. On July 4, 1795, the cornerstone was laid for the building that would establish young Bulfinch's reputation and forever alter the face of old Trimountain.

THE STATE HOUSE

The view below (Figure 7) is one of countless images from the early decades of the nineteenth century, when the Massachusetts State House was among the best known and most admired public buildings in the new nation. Standing majestically on its hillside, the

Figure 7   The State House

State House became the symbol of city and commonwealth, setting the style for public buildings across America. Its facade featured a projecting brick arcade supporting a Corinthian colonnade, the columns carved on the site from giant trees harvested in Maine.

Bulfinch's superb dome was crowned with a gilded pine cone, symbol of the great forests that had enriched the state from colonial days.

The building has undergone many changes: a basement was added and the chimneys removed. The dome, originally shingled and whitewashed, was later clad in copper (with sheets from Paul Revere's mill), then painted gray, and finally in 1874 dressed in its familiar gold leaf (which, as a civil defense measure, was painted black during the Second World War). The brick walls were painted white, then yellow, and then white again before all paint was removed in 1928.

Moreover, as the state government expanded, the seat of government grew accordingly. The once-modest State House has grown tenfold. An addition in 1831 obscured the building's north facade (which originally resembled its front, as pictured on page 15). Subsequent extensions in 1856 and in 1895 added an oversized yellow-brick annex that stretched still farther to the north. Finally, the white marble wings built between 1914 and 1917 provided the familiar frame for a somewhat dwarfed Bulfinch front. Historian Walter Muir Whitehill called the modern State House "a very odd fowl, indeed — with a golden topknot, a red breast, white wings, and a yellow tail."

NEW BEGINNINGS

Symbolically at least, the building of the State House was the beginning of the end of the Trimount, which until this time had suffered surprisingly little physical change. Now, in 1795, it was probably the largest parcel of uninhabited land on the peninsula, and its slopes were being invaded from all sides. From the east, the residential neighborhood facing the harbor had crept up and over the summit of Cotton Hill and advanced to Beacon Street as far as the old Hancock pasture. From the north, a similar encroachment was under way; from the fashionable residential quarter at Bowdoin Square, the streets we know as Bowdoin, Hancock, and Temple marched uphill as far as the sheer north wall of the beacon mound.

The illustrations on these pages are based on a series of rough sketches executed in 1811 by J. R.

Figure 8   The Monument from Temple Street

Smith, an English drawing master then working in Boston. In 1855, Smith's sketches were published as color lithographs, providing a remarkable record of the final days on the old summit. Figure 8 shows the north face of the hill before digging began. This view, from the top of Temple Street, presents a charming scene: the rugged old path, replaced with a flight of stairs built into the hillside, is flanked by a pair of ornamental trees. At the top of the mound the Bulfinch column rises grandly, while the State House dome is just visible behind the crest of the hill.

Figures 9 and 10 chronicle the actual destruction of Beacon Hill. Seen at right is a rare view of the north State House facade, long since obscured by additions to the original structure. As gravel is loaded into horse-drawn carts, the monument perches precariously near the edge of the half-demolished hilltop.

The monument reappears in Figure 10 along with a large and imposing dwelling overlooking today's Bowdoin Street. William Thurston, a prosperous lawyer, had built this house just seven years earlier on land purchased from the Hancock estate. Enjoying one of the finest views in Boston, Thurston's residence sat high on a bank with its western foundation just two feet from the monument lot. Already imperiled in this view, the Thurston house was soon condemned as unsafe and subsequently destroyed.

Recollections gathered a generation later provide a glimpse of the old summit in its final years. It was "of a very peculiar conical shape, and the boys were accustomed to throw their balls up as far as possible towards its summit, which rebounded from it as from a wall." "The sport of batting the ball up the hill and meeting it again on its descent was played by some, but it was not so easy a game as one would at first suppose, on account of the difficulty of maintaining one's footing on the hill side, which was so steep as to require some skill even to stand erect on it."

Over time, the summit's odd, knoblike shape had been accentuated by repeated digging around its base. For decades, there had been complaints of gravel being taken from the sides of the hilltop, and excavations for the State House had cut into the mound's south face. Very soon earth was being moved on all sides as the surrounding slopes were graded for streets and house lots. By 1811 the stability of the old summit had been severely undermined, and it was declared a hazard and an eyesore. Moreover, the town needed money, and the site was valuable both for its gravel and as house lots. Thus, despite mild protests, the land was sold. The monument was dismantled, its gilded eagle and commemorative plaques transferred to the State House. The hill was eventually reduced by some 60 feet to the foundation level of the State House, and

Figure 9   The Destruction of Beacon Hill

the gravel was carted downhill to fill some 50 acres beyond Causeway Street — hence the old quip that North Station is built on the top of Beacon Hill.

This had been a time of intense economic activity. During the war, Boston's population had actually declined. Moreover, the departed Tories counted for many of the town's wealthiest and most prominent citizens. With the 1790s came a period of recovery, then an era of unprecedented prosperity. Old fortunes were revitalized and new ones

Figure 10   The Thurston House

created as the China trade flourished. The population increased almost 30 percent in a single decade (1800-1810). The provincial town of Boston was bursting at the seams and flush with prosperity, and, in the minds of certain speculators, the time was distinctly ripe for ventures in real estate.

THE PROPRIETORS

While the monument was still standing on Beacon Hill, things were astir on the next peak. Beginning in 1799, the western summit had been shorn and smoothed and laid out in house lots — an enterprise of enormous proportions and the work of a real estate syndicate composed of five prominent Bostonians. They called their hill Mount Vernon and took for themselves the name Mount Vernon Proprietors.

The association, which survived for almost thirty years, dramatically changed the aspect of Mount Vernon. The membership also changed from time to time, but the original group consisted of Charles Bulfinch, Jonathan Mason, Harrison Gray Otis, William Scollay, and Joseph Woodward (Figure 11). Bulfinch withdrew early because of financial problems; Scollay and Woodward also left and others took their place, including Hepzibah Swan, a wealthy matron who developed prime properties on Chestnut Street. Otis and Mason, the key figures throughout the venture, were also the most prominent. Both men represented Massachusetts in the U.S. Senate and in Congress, and Otis would later serve three years as mayor of Boston.

MOUNT VERNON

Between 1795 and 1799, the Proprietors bought some 30 acres of land on the south slope of Mount Vernon. No minor task, the scheme required at least four separate purchases as well as costly negotiations to clear more than a dozen disputed titles. The largest and most attractive parcel was the 18 acres belonging to John Singleton Copley — 11 acres in upland pasture and the remainder a soggy tidal "beach" along the western shore.

One of the best known chapters in the history of Beacon Hill concerns the Proprietors' purchase of Copley's pasture. The artist had been living in London since 1774, and it is often hinted that the Proprietors took advantage of his long absence and tricked him into selling his land at too low a price. Copley tried to withdraw from the agreement, which had been executed by his Boston agent, but the contract was declared binding.

Much has been written on this point, with exhaustive research involving masses of material that is sometimes incomplete and often contradictory. In general, investigators have tended to conclude, with a shrug, that Copley was no fool and was in fact aware that his Beacon Hill property was rising in value. It is also pointed out that Copley realized a good profit on his land, receiving more than $18,000 from an investment of $3000. Moreover, in another purchase by the Proprietors at about the same time, eight acres of the old James Allen pasture were acquired for $6100, or about $750 per acre, which makes the Copley purchase price look quite fair.

In any case, Copley withdrew his initial objections and begrudgingly accepted his money, and the Proprietors set about their business. In 1799 they began the actual work of grading, the project that Harrison Gray Otis described as "our great operation."

It was a great operation indeed, and it predictably attracted spectators — young boys and sidewalk superintendents of the day. Otis noted with satisfaction that the Mount Vernon project had "excited as much attention as Bonaparte's road over the Alps." A gravity railroad was constructed, traversing the slope southwesterly from the crest above Louisburg Square to the foot of the hill near Beacon Street. From here, the material removed from the summit was spread out along the shore, creating Charles Street and additional land westward to present-day River Street. The filling of Charles Street was a brilliant stroke: In addition to creating new real estate for development, it established a land route around the western slope of Mount Vernon, previously accessible only by water.

THE PLAN

This cut-and-fill operation continued for three years, during which time the modern street pattern began to emerge. Chestnut and Olive (Mount Vernon) streets were cut through in 1799, Pinckney in 1802. These major east-west routes paralleled the old ridge line. Falling off to the north and south were shorter streets that were almost random in width, length, and placement. Thus, although Beacon Hill's street plan is basically a grid, its effect is considerably more varied, with a small scale and sense of intimacy that are especially appealing.

The author of this plan is not known, but it is considerably more modest than two alternate proposals, one by Charles Bulfinch and the other by surveyor Mather Withington. Both schemes were grandiose, calling for estate-sized properties with large freestanding mansions, private stables, and ample gardens. It has been calculated that if adopted, the Withington plan would have allowed for about 40 dwellings on all the Proprietors' land. The Bulfinch plan, somewhat more modest, might have accommodated 60.

MANSION-HOUSES

About a dozen such houses were built. In 1802 Proprietors Otis and Mason set the style with showpieces on Olive Street. Mason's handsome brick mansion stood high on the hill, opposite the head of

Harrison Gray Otis
by Gilbert Stuart

Jonathan Mason
by Gilbert Stuart

Charles Bulfinch
by Mather Brown

Hepzibah Swan
by Gilbert Stuart

William Scollay
by Edward Greene Malbone

Joseph Woodward
by Mather Brown

Figure 11   The Five Original Mount Vernon Proprietors and Mrs. Swan

Walnut Street(Figure 12). Facing sideways onto a pleasant courtyard, its facade featured a curved central bay, probably the first streetside appearance of the now-familiar Beacon Hill bowfront.

The low building glimpsed behind the mansion is the stable, which stands today as Number 24 Pinckney Street (page 50). Mr. Mason's fine house did not survive, however. It was demolished soon after his death in 1836, and its spacious grounds were carved into house lots for Numbers 59 to 67 Mount Vernon Street and smaller properties on Pinckney Street.

Figure 12   The Mason House

Harrison Gray Otis's Olive Street house, standing today as Number 85 Mount Vernon (page 45), is Beacon Hill's best surviving example of the free-standing mansion-house. It is one of a noble trio of dwellings designed for Otis by Charles Bulfinch. The earliest, built in 1796, stands at 141 Cambridge Street (page 71); the second was the Mount Vernon Street house, which Otis occupied from 1802 to 1806; and the third was the spacious residence at 45 Beacon Street (page 31). Here he lived for more than forty years, holding high office, entertaining the rich and famous, and increasing his private fortune — and generally regarded as one of the most successful and most respected men in Boston.

Of the dozen or so other freestanding mansions built during these years, a few have survived, such as the 1804 Phillips house, now Number 1 Walnut Street (page 29), and the 1803 John Callender house at 14 Walnut (page 43). The Callender house, defined as "a small house for little money," was not built on Proprietors' land. It stands on the northwest corner of a two-acre plot that was owned by Dr. John Joy, the local apothecary who became one of the hill's earliest residents.

Other early mansion-houses have disappeared: the Thomas Perkins house, completed in 1805 at the northeast corner of Dr. Joy's property, which like the Mason house was sacrificed for the value of the land it occupied; and "the finest house on Chestnut Street," the 1804 estate of Richard Crowninshield Derby, which disappeared sometime before 1880 under circumstances that are curiously obscure.

EARLY ROW HOUSES

Given their choice of street plan, it seems unlikely that even the Proprietors envisioned a neighborhood composed exclusively of freestanding houses. From the earliest years of the enterprise, double houses and even larger blocks were built on the Proprietors' land.

Charles Bulfinch designed pairs of freestanding double houses at 6 and 8 Chestnut Street and at 87 and 89 Mount Vernon. The Chestnut Street houses (page 36) featured a circular carriageway leading alongside the buildings to rear stable yards. These houses stood free for about thirty years, until Numbers 4 and 10 were built on the carriageway. Of the Mount Vernon Street houses, Number 87 (page 45) has survived as designed. Its handsome downhill neighbor is the result of extensive reconstructions in the 1870s (when it was given a brownstone facade) and in 1917 (when it was restored to red brick).

Other double houses were always intended to be part of rows. Sometimes as twins and sometimes in mirror image, the double house first appeared during the mansion-house era and continued to be popular. Indeed, some of Beacon Hill's most handsome houses are in pairs, with some of the finest examples on Beacon Street.

Thus, not even the Proprietors were wedded to the freestanding model. Around 1805, Mrs. Swan commissioned Bulfinch to build Numbers 13, 15, and 17 Chestnut Street (page 36), which she gave to her three daughters as wedding presents. Two years later, Jonathan Mason subdivided a lot just east of his own dwelling to erect Numbers 51 through 57 Mount Vernon Street as rental properties. The best

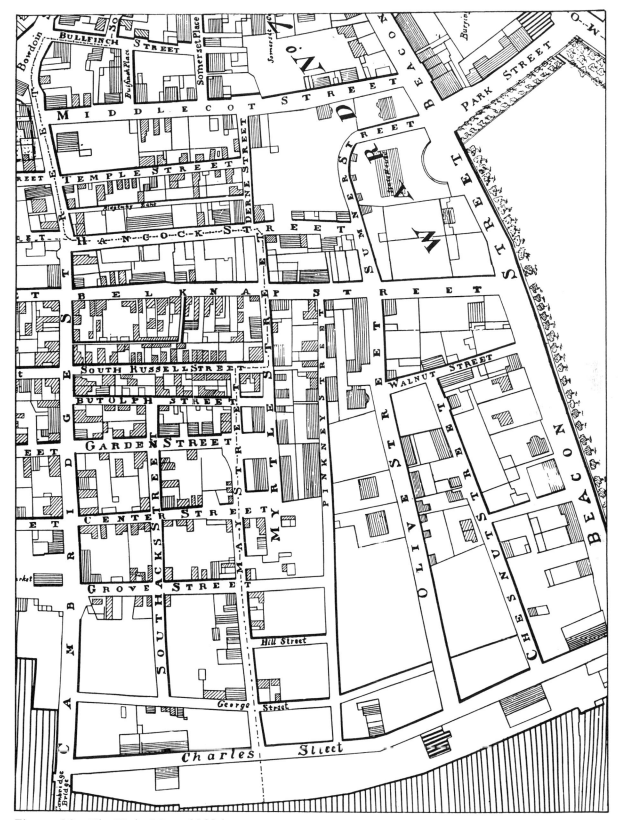

Figure 13   The Hales Map of 1814

Brick

Wood

preserved of this block is Number 55, today the Nichols House Museum (page 43).

The Mount Vernon project was under way. It was a well-satisfied Harrison Gray Otis who wrote to a friend: "We are taking down Mount Whoredom. If in future you visit it with less pleasure you will do so with more profit."

EMBARGO

Just as the Proprietors' venture seemed to be successfully launched, it was halted by a serious national recession stemming from Jefferson's 1807 embargo on trade with Britain and France. The downturn devastated the booming maritime economy of Boston, and for more than a decade — the embargo years and the ensuing War of 1812 — there was very little new construction on Beacon Hill.

Figure 13 presents a detail from an 1814 plan of the city known as the Hales Map, which gives a fairly accurate picture of Beacon Hill during the lull. The modern street pattern is almost complete, and many house lots are occupied — quite a few by houses standing today. However, there is still a generous scattering of vacant lots and some large tracts of open land, especially on the western slope. Particularly interesting is the North Slope, where diagonal hatching indicates the prevalence of wood houses.

Beacon Hill languished in this half-developed state until the late 'teens, and when building resumed, there were several important changes. The freestanding model almost disappeared; among the last of these houses was the 1819 David Sears mansion at 42 Beacon Street (Figure 14). From this time forward houses were built in blocks of nearly identical structures. Moreover, while fine and costly houses continued to be built, the trend was toward more modest dwellings reflecting a less expansive way of life. Private stables, for example, almost disappeared from the residential district. Rather, they were grouped in areas given almost entirely to stabling, such as the north slope of Joy Street and the newly filled land west of Charles Street.

Though new construction lagged, the transformation was well under way. Almost contemporary with the Hales Map is an 1817 letter by a grandiloquent

Figure 14   The Sears Mansion

Bostonian of the day named Shubael Bell. Writing to a boyhood friend who no longer lives in Boston, Bell provides the following account of recent happenings on the Trimountain: "So much of this once elevated spot has been carried to the sea that the tops of chimneys are now so high as the sides were, over which, in your youthful days, you strolled to enjoy the richness of the surrounding scenery."

BOOM AND BUST

Hereafter, the architectural development of Beacon Hill is traditionally broken into three phases. The stylistic characteristics of each period are described elsewhere (pages 116 to 119), but the following paragraphs briefly outline the stages of development of the Beacon Hill row house.

The mansion-house era, so abruptly ended by the embargo, embodied the style known as "Federal" and was dominated by the genius of Charles Bulfinch. When prosperity returned, Bulfinch was out of town, at work on the United States Capitol building in Washington, but his influence lingered. The decade of the '20s saw much activity on the undeveloped parts of the old Copley pasture. Some dwellings were custom built, but most followed the trend toward blocks of houses erected on speculation by builders, or "housewrights." Among the most gifted of these men was Cornelius Coolidge, who was responsible for several blocks of smaller row houses on Chestnut and West Cedar streets (pages 38 and 53).

This transitional decade ended with the Panic of 1829. When building resumed in the early '30s, the Federal style of Bulfinch had given way to the architectural style known as Greek Revival. The ensuing building boom, which was often wildly speculative, focused around upper Mount Vernon Street (which had been renamed in 1832) and in the vicinity of Louisburg Square (seen in Figure 15 around 1850 — with its statuary in place and its central fountain at play).

By 1840, there was little undeveloped land on Beacon Hill, and new building was scattered and limited. In some cases, as on Louisburg Square, the new dwellings honored the spirit of previous decades, but in other cases they displayed an almost revolutionary disregard for tradition. For example, the 1847 double mansions at 70 and 72 Mount

Figure 15 Louisburg Square, circa 1850

Vernon Street (page 46) were built on a scale that almost overwhelmed the great Bulfinch houses across the street. Moreover, they exhibited a bold eclecticism and a break with tradition that announced the arrival of the architectural styles associated with the Victorian era.

Few full-blown Victorian structures were built on Beacon Hill. Nevertheless, the era left its imprint on virtually every street corner. Over several decades residents "updated" their facades with Victorian details and major architectural features such as ornate wooden doorways, mansard roofs, and above all bay windows. The new style found full expression west of Charles Street, on the filled land known locally as the Flat (pages 60-65). Brimmer Street, the district's major residential thoroughfare, displays a pure and robust Victorian flavor.

The story of the next 150 years can be told quickly, because in a sense Beacon Hill has not changed very much. There are notable exceptions, such as the Hancock House, demolished in 1863. Other buildings have undergone considerable change: The Bulfinch-designed Amory-Ticknor House (page 112) at the corner of Beacon and Park streets is sadly altered but still standing, and certainly a prime candidate for renaissance, given its historical credentials. Moreover, the neighborhood abounds with derelict or eccentric architectural relics, altered to meet the demands or the tastes of the times but whose fabric is still viable.

The eastern slope of old Cotton Hill has seen the greatest change. About the only reminder of a more gracious past can be seen at Number 10 1/2 Beacon Street (Figure 16). The Boston Athenaeum, a private library founded in 1807, has occupied this site since 1849, serving as retreat and reading room to generations of Bostonians. The brooding facade is misleading; the picturesque interior was fondly described by local litterateur David McCord as combining "the best elements of the Bodleian, Monticello, the frigate *Constitution,* a greenhouse, and an old New England sitting room."

Cotton Hill was lost through a process of gradual encroachment. In the 1880s half of gracious Pemberton Square was razed to make way for the Suffolk County Courthouse. In fact, the greatest threats to the residential neighborhood have often come from government, especially from state government, whose expansion in the past century has

Figure 16 The Boston Athenaeum

absorbed several acres of Beacon Hill. This trend was happily reversed in 1990, when the State restored a piece of parkland near the site of the original beacon (page 42). Its centerpiece is a granite replica of the Bulfinch Column, which was erected by public-minded citizens in 1898. The northwestern corner of the park was once the site of a huge reservoir (Figure 17) erected in 1848 as part of Boston's first municipal water system.

THE FINAL CHAPTER

The social history of Beacon Hill is a tale of changing fortunes. Perhaps its proudest years were in the middle decades of the nineteenth century, when the district was a recognized center of literary and intellectual activity. Home to philosophers and poets, abolitionists and Transcendentalists, it was witness to and participant in the Flowering of New England, playing host to illustrious visitors including heads of state and royalty. Around 1860, however, Beacon Hill began to lose ground to the Back Bay as the fashionable quarter in town. The challenge was met; as recounted by a Beacon Hill partisan in 1912: "The new

Figure 17   The Beacon Hill Reservoir

inhabitants of the new houses in the new streets toward the west shook their heads and made disparaging remarks concerning antiquity, remoteness, decay, and downfall; but certain old inhabitants

stood firm. . . . Little by little, the novelty of settlement upon the manufactured land wore off, and a younger generation sprang up to rediscover that the Hill had practical advantages together with a definite charm. . . . The fortunate result is that the wide, western slope of the Hill stands now much as it stood in the pleasant days of old, helped rather than impaired by a spruce, almost jaunty air of rejuvenation."

The annals of Beacon Hill abound with similar expressions of loyalty and affection. Indeed, the preservation of the neighborhood has been largely due to the vigilance and care of the people who have lived here. One of the best-known pieces of local lore dates from 1947, when Beacon Hill residents locked horns with the administration of Mayor James Michael Curley over the city's decision to replace the old brick sidewalks with cement. The battle line was drawn on West Cedar Street, where for several days in April Beacon Hill women staged a sit-down demonstration (page 114) upon the bricks they were determined to protect. The mayor backed down.

While Beacon Hill was to suffer subsequent reversals of fortune, it never fell completely from fashion. On the South Slope, some streets always retained a modicum of respectability, while on the North Slope, essentially a melting-pot neighborhood, certain pockets were to flourish as centers of bohemianism. The rush to the suburbs in the 1940s and '50s and the inner-city turmoil of the '60s offered fresh challenges to the stability of the neighborhood.

As early as 1922, Beacon Hill residents had organized to address their common problems. They established the Beacon Hill Civic Association, which since that time has developed an efficient committee system to deal with a full range of neighborhood issues such as traffic and parking, zoning and licensing, trees and sidewalks, public safety, and cleanup. In recent years the BHCA has sparred with large and powerful institutions wishing to expand. Both Suffolk University and Massachusetts General Hospital have displayed territorial ambitions; in both cases, the BHCA has worked out a viable truce.

Among the BHCA's more recent accomplishments has been the inauguration of a resident-sticker program, subsequently adopted by several other

Boston neighborhoods, which reserves most on-street parking spaces for local residents. The association has also been instrumental in developing the labyrinthian traffic pattern, which aims to discourage nonresidential traffic from using Beacon Hill streets. The key to the system is an abundance of one-way streets and almost twice as many roads exiting the neighborhood as those providing entrance.

For more than a century, each generation of homeowners had witnessed the disappearance of a few old buildings, but the attrition was so gradual that it gave little cause for alarm. In the 1950s, however, there was widespread concern that the pressures of development might lead to significant new building, including the new threat of high-rise construction. The BHCA played a key role in initiating legislation creating the Beacon Hill Historic District. Legisla-tion in 1955 included only the 22 acres of the South Slope; the Flat was added in 1958, and the North Slope in 1963. Under the terms of the legislation, no building or part of a building seen from a public way can be altered in any way without approval of a five-member commission. In 1963 the neighborhood was declared a Registered National Historic Landmark.

Harrison Gray Otis apparently predicted that Bea-con Hill would remain a residential quarter because its slopes would be inhospitable for any other use. Here again, Otis's instincts were basically sound. His "Mount Vernon" has survived population shifts and economic reversals to become one of the nation's best-preserved and most admired urban neighbor-hoods — a place of rare ambience and beauty, with its residential character assured.

— GAIL WEESNER

The Beacon, 1720

THE PUBLIC VIEW
Beacon Hill from Above

NORTH

Ashburton Place

Bowdoin Street

Park Street

ASHBURTON PARK

Temple Street

Derne Street

STATE HOUSE

Hancock Street

Cambridge Street

Beacon Street

Mt. Vernon Pl.

Joy Pl.

Joy Street

Smith Ct.

Joy Ct.

Joy Street

Frog Pond

South Russell Street

Pinckney Street

Walnut Street

Irving Street

Myrtle Street

Mount Vernon Street

Chestnut Street

Spruce Ct.

THE COMMON

Garden Street

Rollins Pl.

Revere Street

Spruce St.

Anderson Street

Strong Pl.

Champney Pl.

Phillips Street

Willow St.

Acorn St.

Branch Street

Spruce Street

Grove Street

Louisburg Sq.

Charles Street

Goodwin Pl.

Sentry Hill Pl.

Bellingham Pl.

Cedar Street

Street

Way

River Street

Byron Street

THE PUBLIC GARDEN

The Lagoon

SUBWAY

West

Cedar Lane

Street

Lime Street

Beaver Street

Charles

Cedar

West Hill Pl.

Charles River Sq.

Mt. Vernon Square

Brimmer Street

River Street

Beaver Place

Arlington Street

Longfellow Bridge

Otis Pl.

Storrow Drive

BACK BAY

Charles River Esplanade

Charles River

Hatch Shell

BEACON STREET
"The Sunny Side"

TO MANY MINDS, the name of Beacon Street is synonymous with Boston. The oldest street on Beacon Hill, it was once the colonists' path to the Beacon. Trailing westward toward the water, it formed the boundary between Boston Common and privately owned upland pasture.

The street has always been defined by its proximity to the Common, and it was probably this amenity that led wealthy Bostonians to establish country estates on the hillside. (Two of these early landholders — patriot John Hancock and expatriate John Singleton Copley — would achieve considerable fame.) By 1800, however, this land had become too valuable for such lavish use, and in the ensuing decades Beacon Street became the site of some of the earliest and most elegant town houses of the Federal era.

Until 1821 the street terminated in a dead end near Charles Street, next to the Back Bay waters. In that year it was extended atop the new Mill Dam, which now traversed the mud flats, providing a new route to the mainland at Brookline. Today, Beacon Street winds some ten miles through western suburbs to its conclusion just short of the Newton-Wellesley town line.

The street has always had aristocratic associations. To nineteenth-century wit Oliver Wendell Holmes, it was "the sunny side that holds the sifted few." As a major city thoroughfare, it has suffered more changes than other Beacon Hill streets. Nevertheless, it retains its general air of prosperity and more than a few fine old houses.

NOTED RESIDENTS:

Ralph Waldo Emerson, essayist   Site of Number 10 1/2

Christian A. Herter, statesman   Number 61

Eben Jordan, merchant   Number 46

William Hickling Prescott, historian   Number 55

Charles and Beacon. Beacon Street rises gently toward
the State House, with Boston Common on the right. A
major urban traffic artery, Beacon Street is also a
favored route for footraces and parades.

The Shaw Memorial. Pictured at right, and situated opposite the State House is the Robert Gould Shaw Memorial, a bas-relief by America's foremost nineteenth-century sculptor, Augustus Saint-Gaudens. A mounted Shaw leads the Massachusetts 54th Regiment, the first all-volunteer black regiment in the Union Army. Colonel Shaw, together with many of his officers and men, died at Fort Wagner, South Carolina, in July 1863. Their story was told in the 1990 film Glory.

The State House. The oldest and most prominent structure on Beacon Street is the Massachusetts State House, designed by 24-year-old Charles Bulfinch in 1787 and completed eleven years later. To generations of Americans it was among the most admired public buildings in the nation. Bulfinch's original brick facade has seen many changes and additions, most recently the marble wings built between 1914 and 1917. The gilded pine cone crowning the dome symbolizes the great forests that have enriched the state since its earliest days. Directly beneath the dome is the original House of Representatives room, today's Senate Chamber. Seen at left, this room has undergone periodic alterations but retains much of the fine Federal detail selected by Bulfinch two centuries ago. The rusticated walls are actually made of plaster and date from 1866, when the room's four fireplaces were removed.

33 and 34 Beacon. These two imposing Greek Revival houses, erected in 1825 by housewright Cornelius Coolidge, have both been converted from residential use. Number 33 was bequeathed to the city (along with a large fortune) by George Francis Parkman in 1908. It serves today as the city's official guest house. Number 34 is the headquarters of Little, Brown and Company, publishers. The iron balconies are later additions.

The Phillips House. Built in 1804 by Charles Bulfinch, this was the first brick residence on Beacon Street. The mansion was designed for John Phillips, Boston's first mayor (1822), but is better known as the birthplace of the mayor's abolitionist son Wendell. This Federal-period house once stood free with gardens and stables and a front door at 38 Beacon. When the building was Victorianized, the entry was moved to Walnut Street.

From the Common. The unbroken line of red brick facades presents a unified front. Actually, these houses display far greater diversity than is seen elsewhere on Beacon Hill. This part of Beacon Street began primarily as a collection of freestanding single and double houses, which were connected by later construction. Above Charles Street today, there are no more than two buildings of the same design.

Double Houses. The double house appeared early on Beacon Street and continued as a favored architectural form. Seen on the left, Numbers 54 and 55 (1808, by Asher Benjamin) present a gently bowed double facade in mirror image. With flat Federal entrances, these were the first bowfronts on Beacon Street. On the right are Numbers 39 and 40 (1818, by Alexander Parris). This handsome pair with portico entrances and boldly swelling bays were built as twins; renovations in the 1880s added a fourth floor to both houses and a central set of windows in the bow at Number 39. Here in 1843, Henry Wadsworth Longfellow married Fanny Appleton, whose father built this house.

45 Beacon. The finest mansion-house on Beacon Street, this was Harrison Gray Otis's last home. Like his first two residences (pages 45 and 71), this house was designed by Bulfinch. Completed in 1808, it stood free with a stable yard on the downhill side and an English garden uphill. In 1831, Otis gave up half the garden to build his daughter a brick house (44 Beacon) attached to his own. He sold the other half to his neighbor David Sears, who put up an addition to his own granite mansion (43 Beacon, pictured below). The high granite base and the carved eagle over the window were later embellishments to the house.

The Somerset Club. This imposing granite edifice at 42-43 Beacon Street was built in three stages. The swelled bay to the east was the central feature in a two-story granite house designed for Colonel David Sears by Alexander Parris (see page 20). Dating from 1819, it strikingly resembled the brick mansion built by Sears's father-in-law, Jonathan Mason (page 18, Figure 12). In 1832 Colonel Sears extended his house westward to include a second round bay. Some forty years later, acquired by the Somerset Club, the building was given a third floor. The rusticated granite wall with the massive studded doors was probably added about the same time. It is generally believed that this was the site of the residence of John Singleton Copley.

66 Beacon. At the junction of Beacon and Charles streets is a substantial seven-story building of brick and granite with elaborately carved stone detail. It was erected in 1890 by the New York architectural firm of McKim, Mead and White. One of the neighborhood's first modern apartment buildings, its urbanity is further revealed by the inclusion of commercial space on the ground floor.

King's Chapel House. This is the lower member of another fine pair of bowfronts, 63 and 64 Beacon. These early Greek Revival houses, now the property of King's Chapel, date from the early 1820s and display authentic examples of the much-admired purple windowpanes — a reminder of an error in glass-making. This distinctive coloration appeared after exposure to the sun, which brought out an imperfection in some pieces of window glass manufactured between 1818 and 1825. The houses are subtly individualized. For example, the portico entrance of Number 64, shown here, features columns with Doric capitals while those of its mate are Ionic.

Cheers! The elegant Georgian Revival mansion at 84 Beacon Street was once a private residence. Both exterior and interior were designed by Ogden Codman in 1909. Now known as the Hampshire House, it accommodates a restaurant, a lounge, the "Cheers" bar of television fame, and a spectacular private penthouse overlooking the Public Garden.

70-75 Beacon. This handsome row of six granite town houses was the 1828 design of Asher Benjamin. Because they were erected on filled land, they have sometimes been called the earliest Back Bay houses. In spirit, however, they belong to Beacon Hill, and by modern geography as well, they are Beacon Hill houses. This row provides an excellent example of how once-identical houses, gradually altered by a succession of owners, achieve individuality while remaining part of a group. Extra stories, iron balconies, and wonderfully varied bay windows add character to the ensemble. Number 72 is probably closest to the original design.

CHESTNUT STREET
Harmony Reigns

PROBABLY BEACON HILL'S loveliest street, Chestnut Street was one of the first to be laid out by the Mount Vernon Proprietors, and it was built up quickly. Only a few houses above Charles Street were erected after the 1820s. In general, development occurred from the top downward, with the older and more stately houses near Walnut Street and smaller, later structures near Charles. (The filled land west of Charles Street, for many years the domain of tradesmen and stablers, is considered part of "The Flat," pages 60-65.)

The development of Chestnut Street was thus more unified and more carefully planned than that of other Beacon Hill streets, resulting in a conspicuous harmony of scale and spirit. With its gentle air of quiet respectability, this street, it seems, has also been respected. A bastion of single-family residences, it has seen fewer changes than most streets its age. To many minds, Chestnut Street is the quintessence of Beacon Hill, and it is widely recognized as one of the finest collections of Federal-period domestic architecture in America.

NOTED RESIDENTS:

Edwin Booth, actor Number 29A

Ralph Adams Cram, architect Number 52

Richard Henry Dana, Jr., author Number 43

James Russell Lowell, poet Number 51

Francis Parkman, historian Number 50

Under the Lindens. Stepping gently uphill, these Chestnut Street houses reveal an appealing variety of ornamental details: entryways and windows, brass and ironwork — all combine with streetside gardens and other personal touches to create a dignified yet intimate urban streetscape.

13, 15, and 17 Chestnut. Setting the tone of quiet dignity, this trio is a documented example of the best of Bulfinch. All three, with their adjacent stables on Mount Vernon Street (see page 44), were built between 1806 and 1808 for Mrs. Hepzibah Swan, who herself lived across the street at Number 16. As each of three Swan daughters married, she received one of these houses. Bulfinch signatures include the slender fluted entrance columns, stone string course above recessed brick arches, and tall second-story windows with individual iron balconies.

6 and 8 Chestnut. The design for this early double house is also attributed to Bulfinch. Originally freestanding, the houses were built for Charles Paine, son of Robert Treat Paine, in 1804. The curved flights of steps are brownstone, a material Bulfinch usually used only sparingly. As built, these mirror-matched residences possessed rear stables, approached via a carriageway that circled the houses. By 1820 both the freestanding model and the private stable had been abandoned, and when Cornelius Coolidge purchased the houses he eliminated the carriageway to build Numbers 4 and 10. The houses are now owned by the Society of Friends.

29A Chestnut. This is believed to be the oldest house on Chestnut Street and the first dwelling built by the Mount Vernon Proprietors. Attributed to Bulfinch, it was probably begun in 1799, the year the street was opened. The streetside bow is identified as a later addition by its brickwork (laid in common bond rather than the Flemish bond typical of early construction), and by its lavender windowpanes, known to date from between 1818 and 1825. Its orientation, with its narrow end facing the street, occurs occasionally elsewhere on Beacon Hill. Here, it allows for a charming green garden.

27 Chestnut. This Gothic limestone structure was completed in 1918 as the chapel for Boston University's School of Theology, whose classrooms occupied the buildings at 70-72 Mount Vernon Street (page 46). In 1965 the entire complex was converted to apartments. This is the site of the 1804 Richard Crowninshield Derby mansion, said to have been the grandest house on Beacon Hill.

Housewrights. The pattern of Chestnut Street development is quite clear. The style was set by the Mount Vernon Proprietors led by Charles Bulfinch, but the task was largely completed by housewrights. These entrepreneurial craftsmen/tradesmen are an interesting but elusive group. Though some of them were extremely talented, they never claimed the title "architect," and many are known only by name. Represented on this page are several housewrights who were active on Chestnut Street. The most prolific of the group was Cornelius Coolidge. While he worked on almost every street on Beacon Hill, his most characteristic and most engaging work is here on lower Chestnut Street (above) and around the corner on West Cedar.

Above to the left is a portion of a row erected in the mid 1820s by housewrights Joseph Lincoln and Hezekiah Stoddard, who worked in partnership for more than 20 years. Number 64, the central building in this view, was Stoddard's own home, while Lincoln lived at Number 62.

At left, the gray Federal facade dating from 1809 represents the work of an earlier housewright, Jeremiah Gardner, who was active on other streets and seems to have specialized in double houses. Shown here is Number 23 Chestnut, one of the most admired facades on the street. Its twin at Number 25 has been altered beyond recognition. The gray paint on this and other Federal-period houses continues a practice begun by Charles Bulfinch as a means of waterproofing the porous bricks of the time.

Iron, brass, lead. Nowhere on Beacon Hill does one encounter such stylish variety of ornamentation as on Chestnut Street. Brass is rubbed to a high polish. Leaded-glass windows exhibit a lively variation in pattern, from simple radiating bars to elaborate tracery. Ornamental ironwork adds a vibrant chiaroscuro of silhouette and shadow against a backdrop of stone and brick. Wrought- and cast-iron elements, sometimes original features, were in other cases added by subsequent owners to individualize their homes.

MOUNT VERNON STREET

The Proprietors' Choice

FOLLOWING THE ORIGINAL RIDGELINE of the Trimount, Mount Vernon Street was known as Olive Street until 1832. Above Walnut Street, it is very old — quite possibly following one of Boston's legendary cowpaths — but its western descent was not graded until 1802.

The north side of this new street was soon divided among the Mount Vernon Proprietors, with the apparent intent that each would erect an impressive residence to spur further development. Only two such houses were actually built: Harrison Gray Otis's second house at Number 85 (seen opposite) and the Jonathan Mason residence farther uphill. Both were elegant mansion-houses, freestanding on spacious grounds. The land between these two showpieces remained vacant until the 1830s and then developed in the row-house mode, preserving the 30-foot setback that gives this part of the street its distinctive front lawns.

Mount Vernon is Beacon Hill's broadest and greenest street, and its mature elms are as much a part of the streetscape as its fine old houses. Halfway down the hill is Louisburg Square, one of the most admired urban spaces in the nation. This enclosed private park ringed with stately brick dwellings epitomizes the expansive character of the 1830s on Beacon Hill.

NOTED RESIDENTS:
The Adams family (Charles Francis, Charles Francis II, Henry) Number 57
Robert Frost, poet Number 88
Julia Ward Howe, author Number 32
The James family (Alice, Henry, William) Number 131
Henry Cabot Lodge (the elder), statesman Site of Number 65
Maurice and Charles Prendergast, artists Number 60
Daniel Webster, statesman Number 57

Mansion-houses. Set back above the street, the stately mansions of the Mount Vernon Proprietors give just a hint of the Proprietors' vision. By the 1830s, the swell-front house on the right had become the standard for elegant urban living. Henry James called Mount Vernon "the only respectable street in America."

Ashburton Park. The original summit of Beacon Hill stood some 60 feet above this site, in the vicinity of the double stairway leading to the State House annex. In recent memory this was a dreary macadam parking lot for state officials. In the late 1980s a major dig created an underground garage, and this welcoming green park was dedicated in the spring of 1991. The central feature is an 1898 replica of the 1789 "Bulfinch Column," removed when the hill's summit was lowered in 1811.

1-5 Joy Street (south of Mount Vernon Street corner). These stately bowfronts resemble houses on Mount Vernon Street and in the vicinity of Louisburg Square. The row was built by Cornelius Coolidge in the mid-1830s. The 15-foot setback recalls an 1805 mansion on the Mount Vernon Street corner, the residence of Thomas Perkins. Bulfinch, the architect, put the drawing rooms in the rear of this house, overlooking the Common. The placement of the Joy Street houses is in accordance with a deed restriction that aimed to preserve Mr. Perkins's view.

The Lyman House. Numbered 6 Joy Street, this substantial brick building is one of eclecticism. Designed by Alexander Parris for George Williams Lyman in 1824, it combines Federal and Greek Revival features with a multitude of window shapes and sizes in asymmetrical arrangement.

The Callender House. This pleasantly domestic gray dwelling at 14 Walnut Street was the first house to be built on Mount Vernon Street. Erected in 1803 by John Callender, it once fronted on Mount Vernon. Its Federal exterior is sheathed with butt-joined boards — a rare example of a once-common treatment.

The Nichols House Museum. The Bulfinch house at 55 Mount Vernon Street is named for its last owner, lifelong resident, and benefactor, Miss Rose Standish Nichols. It was built in 1804 for Jonathan Mason and faced Mason's own splendid mansion just beyond the front garden (see page 18). Incised in the stone string course above the corner window, "Mount Vernon" is not a street sign — the street was called Olive Street until 1832. It proclaims the recently adopted name of the Proprietors' new housing development.

Stables by Bulfinch. Built behind the Chestnut Street Swan houses, these converted stables are numbered 50, 56, and 60 Mount Vernon Street. They have probably survived because of a deeded 13-foot height restriction for any structure built on the site. Beyond the arched double door a wooden cattle ramp still leads to the former stable yard— now terraced gardens. The American Impressionist painter Maurice Prendergast and his brother Charles had their studios here one hundred years ago, when the structures were less well manicured than today (see page 114).

59 Mount Vernon Street. Widely acclaimed as the high point of the Greek Revival style in Boston, this entrance portico has been described as a temple in miniature. The house, built in 1837, was designed by Edward Shaw, a local architect who, like Asher Benjamin, wrote architectural primers. For many years the home of Atlantic Monthly *editor Thomas Bailey Aldrich, it is one of five houses built on the Jonathan Mason estate.*

The Second Otis House. With its lordly setting and overall sense of grandeur, the house at 85 Mount Vernon Street comes closer than any other to capturing the spirit of the mansion-house era. Harrison Gray Otis moved to this house in 1802 and lived here for five years before settling permanently on Beacon Street (page 31). The dominant features of the Bulfinch facade are the recessed parlor-floor windows and two-story Corinthian pilasters. The iron balconies of Chinese fretwork can also be seen on Otis's Beacon Street house. The original property extended northward to Pinckney Street. Though this rear acreage was sold for house lots in the 1830s, the house retains its cobbled carriageway, courtyard, and stables.

87 Mount Vernon. The surviving member of an 1806 pair, this house was built by Bulfinch on land that he himself owned. The suggestion that the architect intended it for his own residence has never been verified; perhaps this plan fell victim to Bulfinch's chronic financial woes. In any case, by the time the twin dwellings were completed, Number 87 had been sold to Boston banker Stephen Higginson, Jr. Contemporary with the Third Otis House (page 31), this structure has much in common with the Beacon Street mansion — though its four-bay facade precludes a symmetrical treatment. Since 1955 it has housed the headquarters of the Colonial Society of Massachusetts.

Setback. Between the Otis House and the site of the Mason estate, the Mount Vernon Street houses stand 30 feet back from the street. This setback is reputedly based on an early gentlemen's agreement among the Proprietors to establish and preserve the elegant character of the new street. The 1830s row houses respected this agreement, and their ample front yards are today embellished with pleasant gardens and an exuberant display of ornamental cast iron.

70-72 Mount Vernon. These monumental brownstones were built in 1847 for brothers John and Nathaniel Thayer. Designed by Richard Upjohn, they represent an early and daring break with tradition. (Upjohn, known as a Gothic Revivalist, designed Trinity Church in New York.) For many years the buildings were used as Boston University's School of Theology, connected internally to the Gothic chapel at 27 Chestnut Street (page 37). After a time as a pharmacy school, the complex was developed as apartments, then converted to condominiums.

Louisburg Square. This well-known place is generally considered the heart of Beacon Hill. The cobbled road and oval park are owned and maintained by the abutting householders, including those on Pinckney Street. The square was created in 1826 as one of the last acts of the Mount Vernon Proprietors before dividing their holdings, and the houses were built between 1835 and 1847. The statues of Aristides and Columbus (below) arrived in 1850. Italian in origin, they were the gift of Joseph Iasigi, a Mediterranean merchant who lived at Number 3. In addition to the massive cast-iron fence enclosing the park, the square displays various examples of more delicate work. Below is a section of the balcony at Numbers 1-3, with wrought-iron serpents whose twisted tongues form flagpole holders.

PINCKNEY STREET
"Noble Bohemianism"

PINCKNEY STREET once formed the northern boundary of the Mount Vernon Proprietors' land, and for much of its history the street performed this marginal function, standing guard on the outer edge of respectability. Indeed, the long, uninterrupted roadway of upper Pinckney was probably considered a buffer between the Proprietors' prime real estate and the somewhat scruffy neighborhood to the north. However, this configuration was also determined by the presence, until 1805, of long ropewalks between Pinckney and Myrtle streets, beginning near Hancock Street and descending westward to the vicinity of Grove.

Upper Pinckney Street displays a cheerfully eclectic character that reflects a haphazard pattern of development. Here are found eighteenth-century wooden cottages, one of the earliest blocks of row houses on Beacon Hill, and even a converted stable, all coexisting with Greek Revival development houses and Victorian (and Victorianized) structures of every size and description. Below Anderson, the street assumes a tidier aspect, reflecting its approach to Louisburg Square.

Sociologically as well, the street has always steered its own course. From an early date it displayed a character once styled as "noble bohemianism." As revealed by the illustrious names listed below, it has tended to attract the literati, some as long-term residents and others as itinerants. Today, because most of its houses are modest in size, it is a family street with a large number of one-family dwellings.

NOTED RESIDENTS:

Louisa May Alcott, author Number 20

John Cheever, author Number 6

Nathaniel Hawthorne, author Number 54

Elizabeth Peabody, educator maintained kindergarten at site of Number 15

Henry David Thoreau, philosopher Number 4

At the crest. The glory of Pinckney Street is its view. Just a few steps beyond this point, the street plunges downward, with a stunning vista (and spectacular sunsets) year round. In springtime, with the pear trees in bloom, it provides one of the most popular sights in Boston. The summit of old Mount Vernon was located just behind the houses on the left.

Upper Pinckney Street. The pictures on this page illustrate the happy architectural jumble that comprises the upper end of Pinckney Street.

The low gray structure pictured above is a survivor. Dating from 1802, it is the original stable for Jonathan Mason's long-departed Mount Vernon Street mansion (page 18). Numbered 24 Pinckney Street, it later became a grocery store, and in 1884 it was converted to domestic use by architect William Ralph Emerson, a cousin of Ralph Waldo. Mr. Emerson's whimsy has not lost its appeal. From the eyebrow on the roof to the tinted bullseye pane in the front door, no two windows of the facade are the same —thus its affection-ate name, the House of Odd Windows.

Below, sandwiched between later brick buildings, is a tiny clapboard house that is counted among the oldest on Beacon Hill. Known as the Middleton-Glapion House, it was erected around 1790 by two black men of those names. Seen on the opposite page is another early house, Number 17, painted green and standing sideways to the street. Its flat brick facade features a Federal-period doorway installed in the 1960s. Other-wise, the house is embellished with an abundance of high Victorian features. The prominent bay window sets the style for the rest of the street — Pinckney Street between Joy and Charles streets is overlooked by no fewer than 50 bay windows — Victorian additions, which would be disallowed today under the restrictions of the Historic District Act (see page 23).

65 Anderson Street (corner of Pinckney). While this building is reminiscent of Bulfinch and Benjamin, its architect is unknown. It was erected in 1824 as the first permanent home of English High School. Twenty years later it became a neighborhood grammar school, which in 1855 was one of the first city schools to be integrated. Later it housed a small technical college, and in 1983 was converted to condominiums. The cupola, an original feature, was rebuilt at that time.

Patriarchs. Extending uphill from the corner of Anderson, eight Federal-period houses comprise one of the earliest rows on Beacon Hill. These houses date from around 1810, and there is internal evidence that at least some of them were once only three stories tall. This row provides another example of how dwellings that were once similar have been individualized. In the foreground, Number 51 features a large bay window, the house next door has small iron balconies, and so on down the row.

WEST CEDAR STREET
Quiet Distinction

WEST CEDAR STREET is one of the few streets that run across the hill rather than up and down, and its grade is almost level. A gentle slope is nicely complemented by an equally gentle curve at the Revere Street corner. Just a short block from busy Charles Street, West Cedar sets a tone of quiet distinction that echoes in nearby streets.

The street also shows evidence of good planning. Each block has its own character — one might almost say its own decade. The block between Chestnut and Mount Vernon streets (opposite) derives much of its character from the 1827 row by Cornelius Coolidge. With arched entryways, lovely fanlights, and ground-floor triple windows, these houses are late Federal in spirit. The next block is emphatically of the 1830s, dominated by the flat-headed portals of the Greek Revival period. Between Pinckney and Revere streets the houses of the 1840s become more modest with the approach of the architecturally "marginal" block north of Revere — a typical North Slope mixture of tenement buildings and earlier structures.

In a sense, both West Cedar Street and its service alley, Cedar Lane Way, terrace the hill's western slope. The houses are literally built into the hillside. Thus, dwellings on the west side of the street have basement floors opening onto gardens, while gardens on the other side of the street are buttressed with raised terraces. West Cedar Street has two appendages, Cedar Lane Way and Acorn Street. Both are short, straight, and picturesque, functioning as service alleys as well as residential ways.

NOTED RESIDENTS:
Asher Benjamin, architect Number 9
John P. Marquand, author Number 43
Wendell Phillips, orator Number 24

West Cedar and Chestnut. The ornamental iron lyre set into a former window opening identifies the clubhouse of the Harvard Musical Association, founded in 1837 to stimulate local interest in choral, symphonic, and chamber music. Beyond is the much-admired row of houses erected by Cornelius Coolidge in 1827.

7, 9, 11 West Cedar. In contrast to their Federal-style neighbors across the street, these three houses are forthrightly Greek Revival. Built in 1835, all have been attributed to Asher Benjamin. Number 9 was the noted architect's home. All are fine examples of Benjamin's precise intentions — simple flat-headed doorways and dignified parlor-floor windows behind an elaborate cast-iron balcony.

Acorn Street. The most photographed street in town, tiny Acorn Street is, like Louisburg Square, cobbled and privately owned. This row of nine houses was erected in 1828 and 1829, again by Cornelius Coolidge, perhaps for the coachmen and other retainers of the big houses on Mount Vernon and Chestnut streets. In 1991 the cobbles were removed for utility work. Fiercely protected by residents, these stones were put in storage and when work was completed, they were painstakingly relaid.

Cedar Lane Way. One of the narrowest streets in Boston, Cedar Lane Way provides a service alley for West Cedar Street residents. The small houses on the west side of the lane may have been built as homes and workshops for the many craftsmen and carpenters clustered in this area in the 1820s and 1830s, when Beacon Hill was abuilding. The street was originally paved with oak blocks, some of which survived until recent years.

23 West Cedar. This 1836 house and the adjoining residence at Number 25 were built by Asher Benjamin and housewright Melzar Dunbar. It seems likely that Benjamin was the architect. In fact, the design of the cast-iron balconies appears in Benjamin's 1833 Practice of Architecture. *This pattern of alternating palmettes and lotus blossoms was a favored Greek Revival motif. Like the Greek-key-and-Chinese-fretwork pattern, it recurs at various Beacon Hill addresses.*

CHARLES STREET
Main Street

ONCE THE WATER'S EDGE, Charles Street is built on land brought down from the vicinity of Louisburg Square when the hill's western slope was graded between 1803 and 1805. The street provided a much-needed land route around the base of the hill, and it also created many new house lots on both sides of the new roadway.

In its earliest years the street was mostly residential, but its character was probably always mixed. We know the area was headquarters for the scores of builders and craftsmen who established shops and homes close to the focus of construction activity. The street was also a natural thoroughfare, providing a link to Cambridge by carriage or horse-drawn trolley via the West Boston Bridge, precursor to the 1907 Longfellow Bridge. By the time the trolleys were electrified around 1900, they were sharing the street with early motor cars.

With passing years automobile traffic increased, and by 1920 the old road was considered inadequate. The subsequent widening operation badly mauled the west side of Charles Street and required moving the Meeting House (opposite) ten feet westward. On its uphill side, the street retains some old buildings of both Federal and Greek Revival style.

Charles Street is main street for Beacon Hill residents. Here is the specialty butcher and the gourmet baker (the candlestick maker has disappeared, but in his place are an enticing array of antique shops), and purveyors of essential goods and services, including all manner of eating places. Commercial at sidewalk level, the street has a sizable residential population in apartments and studios on the floors above.

NOTED RESIDENTS:

John Albion Andrew, governor　Number 110

J. T. Fields, publisher　Number 148 (demolished)

Oliver Wendell Holmes, essayist　Number 164　(demolished)

*The Meeting House. Presiding over the modern
commercial scene, the Charles Street Meeting House has
been a landmark since it was built by Asher Benjamin
in 1807. It has survived both a move (ten feet westward
in the 1920s) and a 1982 conversion to office and
retail use. Beyond, Charles Street curves eastward
around the foot of the hill.*

58　　B E A C O N　 H I L L

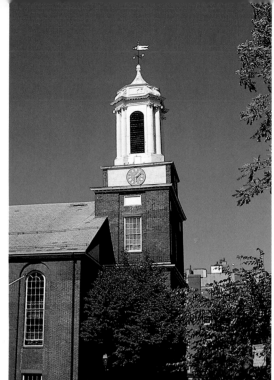

THE FLAT
"The Horsey End of Town"

T H E   M A D E   L A N D west of Charles Street was created after 1850, and well into the twentieth century this was largely a stable area. Its turn-of-the-century character is delightfully portrayed by historian (and lifelong Brimmer Street resident) Samuel Eliot Morison. In *One Boy's Boston,* he recalled that "ours was the horsey end of town . . . occupied by stables big and little — livery stables . . . boarding and baiting stables . . . club stables . . . private stables. Chestnut Street between Charles and the river was called 'Horse-Chestnut' street in derision."

Morison's Brimmer Street was then the only major residential street on the Flat. Pictured opposite, it was constructed at the same time as parts of the Back Bay. Indeed, both geographically and architecturally this area is akin to the Back Bay — but it has always been considered part of Beacon Hill.

Beyond the Victorian domesticity of Brimmer Street, the district offers a variety of residential modes, from converted mews to large and modern apartment complexes. Among the most attractive areas are two twentieth-century Georgian-Revival squares, Charles River Square (1909) and West Hill Place (1916). In Mount Vernon Square, a residential enclave between Charles and Brimmer streets, is a small private park. An American Elm growing nearby is said to be one of the largest such trees in the nation.

NOTED RESIDENTS:
Louis Brandeis, jurist 6 Otis Place
Admiral Richard E. Byrd, explorer 9 Brimmer Street
Edward Filene, merchant 12 Otis Place
Samuel Eliot Morison, historian 44 Brimmer Street

*Brimmer Street. Victorian respectability characterizes
this tree-lined section of Brimmer Street. The houses
in this block were built between 1867 (Number 9)
and 1888 (Number 5). Before construction of the
Esplanade in 1931, the buildings to the west were
riverside properties.*

Eccentrics. More than a century separates the two houses pictured above. On the left is 130 Mount Vernon Street, the inimitable "Sunflower Castle," an 1878 remodeling of an earlier structure. This Bavarian conceit of stucco, tile, and timber has been lovingly maintained by a sequence of owners. Behind the yellow wall on the right nestles one of the oldest of Beacon Hill's "Hidden Gardens." On Beaver Place is another remodeling, the 1983 Deutsch House (right). Atop the original red brick carriage house (which still retains space for a garage), the second-floor addition echoes, in contemporary terms, the style and spirit of the nineteenth-century Sunflower House.

44 Brimmer Street. Behind the ivy at left is the ancestral home of Samuel Eliot Morison, who was born in this house in 1887 and lived here most of his life. It was built in 1870 by Morison's maternal grandfather, Samuel Eliot, on family land inherited by his wife, a granddaughter of Harrison Gray Otis. The historian's short personal memoir, One Boy's Boston, *offers warm and intimate glimpses of the internal workings of this household in turn-of-the-century Boston. As an investment, the Eliots built six additional houses on the remainder of their Otis land, three around the corner on Mount Vernon Street and three across the street on Otis Place (see page 112).*

Church of the Advent. At the corner of Mount Vernon and Brimmer streets (right) is this distinctive High Victorian Gothic structure designed by parishioner John H. Sturgis in 1877 and consecrated in 1894. The exquisite Lady Chapel was the inspiration of another parishioner, Ralph Adams Cram, architect of New York's Cathedral of Saint John the Divine. In the 172-foot tower are carillon bells that were cast and hung by the famed Whitechapel Bell Foundry of London, makers of Big Ben and the Liberty Bell. The parish, formed in 1844, brought the high-church Oxford Movement to Boston. The reredos above the high altar was given to the church by John L. Gardner and his wife, Isabella Stewart Gardner.

165 Mount Vernon. This fine Victorian dwelling (pictured below) dates from 1869. It was designed by William Robert Ware and Herbert Van Brunt, whose best-known work in the Boston area is Harvard's Memorial Hall. Both architects had studied in the New York studios of William Morris Hunt, and their Boston firm was also a teaching studio. In 1865, Ware founded the school of architecture at M.I.T. Here on Brimmer Street, the architects created a brick and brownstone residence of grand proportions. With the extensive use of brownstone, the panel-brick detail, and the great mansard roof, this house is architecturally akin to its contemporaries in the Back Bay.

Sculptural flourish. Below, a reclining figure surveys lower Chestnut Street from an arched niche at Number 90. The house, once a stable, was renovated in 1926 by Henry Sleeper.

14 Byron Street. The Lower Chestnut Street neighborhood contains frequent reminders of its origins as a livery area. The lintel over the carriageway at 14 Byron Street (right) proudly recalls this past. Above, a handsome detail adorns an arched bay of another Byron Street carriage house.

Charles River Square. The early twentieth century saw several developments that extended the character of nineteenth-century Beacon Hill onto the Flat. Below is a view of the 1909 neo-Georgian enclave known as Charles River Square. These riverside houses were once separated from the Esplanade by only a narrow roadway. These pleasant circumstances ended with the construction of Storrow Drive between 1949 and 1951. Nevertheless, Charles River Square and neighboring West Hill Place retain a distinct sense of tranquility.

107 Chestnut Street. At first glance this Mediterranean-style stucco dwelling seems out of place on the banks of the Charles. However, it has stood here since 1913, when it was constructed for Miss Grace Nichols from plans by William Chester Chase. Miss Nichols was a friend of Isabella Stewart Gardner, and this 23-room Chestnut Street residence reflects the spirit of Mrs. Gardner's Fenway Court. Converted to five condominiums in 1981, the building retains many of its baronial features, including magnificent antique oak paneling and mantelpieces gathered in Europe and built into the mansion as it was constructed.

River House. In size, scale, and spirit, this multi-unit apartment house made a bold break with the past. With its light-colored bricks and multiple balconies, it was erected at 145 Pinckney Street in 1951. For local preservationists, this was a call to arms, underscoring the need to protect the neighborhood from similar development. Yet forty years later, River House is undeniably a neighborhood asset, providing a large number of comfortable one-bedroom and studio apartments. In the mid-1980s the building was converted to condominiums.

THE NORTH SLOPE
Potpourri

SO VARIED IS ITS fabric and so rich its history, the North Slope could be given a book of its own. It began as a separate settlement known as West Boston, a small seafaring community nestled near the waterfront. Expanding up the hill, it developed an unsavory reputation that persisted until 1823, the year Mayor Josiah Quincy personally led a series of raids upon the district's undesirable activities. This crusade was apparently successful, and for many years the North Slope was a quieter place. Greek Revival row houses appeared, some erected by the Mount Vernon Proprietors, who had bought up North Slope land as early as 1800.

At the same time, parts of the district had became home to Boston's all-free black community, which had its own church (1806) and school (1835) and whose small frame houses crowded the ways and byways of the steep northern hillside. As the nineteenth century progressed, the area became a center of antislavery activity. The era is commemorated by the Museum of Afro American History, 46 Joy Street.

Beginning around midcentury, blacks began leaving the area for the South End and Roxbury. Across the North Slope, older single-family houses were razed to make way for tenement housing. Near Cambridge Street, this part of Beacon Hill became architecturally and sociologically part of the immigrant quarter known as the West End. In 1898 the African Meeting House was converted to a synagogue, and in 1919 an orthodox congregation, the Vilna Shul, was established on Phillips Street.

NOTED RESIDENTS:

Charles Bulfinch, architect Bulfinch Place (site of the present Saltonstall building)

John Fitzgerald Kennedy, U.S. President 122 Bowdoin Street

Robert Lowell, poet 91 Revere Street

Charles Sumner, statesman 20 Hancock Street

Elihu Yale, benefactor Born in the vicinity of Pemberton Square

Cityscape. Plunging downhill, Anderson Street offers an open view of the Bulfinch Pavilion and Ether Dome of Massachusetts General Hospital (1818-1823). On the right are a striking collection of the "tin bays" that individual-ize the late-nineteenth-century tenement buildings.

Sentry Hill Place. Branching off Revere Street are several small and intimate residential cul-de-sacs. Known as Bellingham, Goodwin, Sentry Hill, and Rollins places, these enclaves were built in the 1840s. Each terminates with a picturesque flourish, like the pair of Greek Revival doorways at the end of Sentry Hill Place. Just a few feet beyond these doors, the hill falls off precipitously, dropping some 30 feet to a parking lot behind Phillips Street (see photo on page 73).

43 South Russell Street. A leading candidate for Beacon Hill's oldest house, this painted brick dwelling was built around 1797 for Joseph Ditson. It was originally freestanding on a much larger lot. The history of this building is meticulously documented in Allen Chamberlain's 1924 book on Beacon Hill. For some time it was a double house and later became a bakery. Today a single-family residence, it retains its original basement kitchen, with bake oven. Wide on the street, this house is only one room deep.

The William C. Nell House. Picturesque Smith Court contains an important cluster of old frame houses. It is also closely linked to local black history. The large clapboard house at Number 3, which strikingly resembles a New England farmhouse, was built about 1800 as a double house with a common entryway. At midcentury, as a boarding house, it was home to William C. Nell, the first published black historian in America.

The African Meeting House and Smith School. The oldest black church building in America, the meeting house, below left, was completed in 1806 — the same year as Asher Benjamin's Old West Church (page 71). Some believe that Benjamin was also involved in this design. From 1898 to 1972 this building was a synagogue, and today it is the centerpiece of the Museum of Afro American History. On the right is the Abiel Smith School, built in 1835 and serving black children from all parts of the city until the Boston schools were integrated twenty years later.

Hill House. The brick building at 74 Joy Street (right) has a distinctly institutional character. Built in 1862 as Station 3 of the Boston Police Department, it became a community center in the late 1960s. Subsequent renovations included converting the old cell block to a gymnasium. Offering programs to residents of all ages, Hill House today is landlord to the Beacon Hill Civic Association and the Beacon Hill Nursery School.

The North-East Slope. In contrast to the other North Slope streets, Hancock, Temple, and Bowdoin streets retain a hint of the opulence and elegance of the once-fashionable Bowdoin Square district. Hancock Street alone provides a capsule history of nineteenth-century Boston domestic architecture, from severe flat-front Federal (Numbers 11 to 23) to 1960s modern (Number 34), including an Egyptian Revival mansion (opposite) and the city's first marble-fronted town houses, Numbers 31 to 37, dating from 1859 and seen below. The houses are attributed to Jonathan Preston, who with his son William would be very active in the early development of Back Bay.

Egyptian Revival. This large and unusual 1875 house at 57 Hancock Street demands attention. Its mansard roof belongs to the tradition of the French Second Empire, but the dormer pylons and the papyrus capitals capping the entrance columns are distinctly Egyptian in origin. The house was designed by William Washburn, best known as an architect of luxury hotels, including the famed Revere House.

The Mission Church of Saint John the Evangelist. The undressed granite edifice at 35 Bowdoin Street was designed in 1831 by Solomon Willard, whose most conspicuous local work is the Bunker Hill Monument. With a square tower and crenellated roofline, it was built for the Congregational Society. It housed the Church of the Advent from 1864 to 1883, when that congregation moved to Brimmer Street.

Side by side. On Cambridge Street are two buildings of architectural distinction. On the left is the first Harrison Gray Otis House, built by Charles Bulfinch in 1796. The only surviving eighteenth-century mansion in the city, it was badly deteriorated when acquired in 1916 as headquarters for the Society for the Preservation of New England Antiquities (see page 114). When Cambridge Street was widened ten years later, the house was rolled back 40 feet. Next door is Asher Benjamin's 1806 Old West Church. With changing times, the congregation dwindled, and in 1892 the church was closed. For more than 70 years it served as the West End Branch of the Boston Public Library.

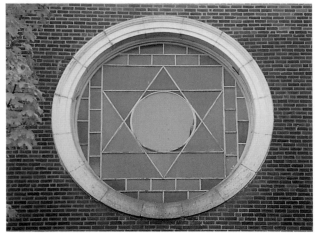

AN INTERIOR VIEW
Inside an Asher Benjamin Town House

The following pages provide a glimpse into some private homes on Beacon Hill. Here we offer a brief discussion of the "typical" town house — its history, its primary features, and the way it was used both then and now.

The hundreds of row houses within the Beacon Hill Historic District vary in size, age, and degree of elegance, both inside and out. Thus, it seems advisable to focus this discussion on a single house. Our search for a prototype was difficult, however, because no existing house is either typical or pure. Because these houses have been lived in, they have been frequently updated in terms of both fashion and technology. Therefore, we soon abandoned the idea of either choosing an existing building as a prototype or concocting one.

Rather, we selected a set of plans from Asher Benjamin's popular *American Builder's Companion,* reprinted six times between 1806 and 1827. This choice seemed appropriate because Benjamin both worked and lived on Beacon Hill. In *American Builder's Companion,* Benjamin published plans for three different types of town houses; here we reprint his drawings for a medium-sized dwelling. Measuring 25 by 37 feet, it contains 3700 square feet of floor space — a middling-to-large Beacon Hill house. The plans present the most common arrangement of rooms in a house three windows wide.

The town house is so totally oriented toward the street that one tends to view a block of houses as a series of facades. However, in nineteenth-century Boston most domestic activities were conducted

through back doors, and the street pattern of Beacon Hill is supplemented by a busy secondary grid of service alleys and footpaths leading to the yards and back entries of almost every house on Beacon Hill. Thus, in order to understand the intimate workings of our Asher Benjamin town house, we will enter the dwelling via the back door.

Pausing in the back yard, we find a miscellaneous clutter of domestic necessities and by-products: an outhouse, a trash pit, a wood pile, and some laundry lines, a rain barrel or cistern, and in some cases a well. The yard functions as a service area for the kitchen, which we now approach.

This is a large, open room with cooking and laundry equipment built into the far wall. The years 1800 to 1840 witnessed great advances in domestic technology, but throughout this house, one finds little evidence of real modernism. Heated by open-hearth fires and lighted by candles and oil lamps, the house has no running water.

Leaving the kitchen, we now go to the front part of the house. En route, we will encounter a discreetly closed door between the front and back halls. While Benjamin's plans do not indicate the presence of any doors, almost every opening would have one, allowing each room to be closed off for efficient heating as well as for privacy.

The front room is identified as a breakfast or counting room, used for informal family meals or serving the man of the house as an office. Just inside the front door and communicating with no other part of the house, it is also a convenient place to receive guests.

Stepping back into the front hall, we find that despite its limited dimensions, every effort has been made to give this area a sense of elegance. The mahogany banister, terminating in a stylized scroll, is rubbed to a high polish; woodwork and cornices are tastefully decorative, designed to make a favorable impression on anyone entering the house.

Arriving at the second-floor landing, we enter the front parlor. This room and its twin in the rear are the finest rooms in the house. They are separated by double sliding doors, allowing the entire area to be used as one room or two. These areas are spacious (15' 6" x 17') with high ceilings. Moreover, they are given identical architectural treatment, from mantelpieces to woodwork and paneling. Though the rear room is designated as a dining room, the two rooms can function as a double parlor. When food is served on this floor, it is carried up the service stairs.

The tiny library at the front of the house seems to be a curious feature. However, private book collections are relatively small, and books are probably considered out of place in a formal parlor.

The front staircase terminates at the parlor-floor level, so to reach the chamber floor we climb the winding back stairs. On the third-floor landing are entrances to three bedchambers; the largest, with an adjoining dressing room, is in the rear. This is probably the master bedroom. Both this room and the front "spare chamber" have a fireplace and a shallow closet, while the smaller front chamber has neither. Presumably the comfortable spare chamber can be used by guests. These rooms are simple and functional, with lower ceilings and little decorative detail.

Though Benjamin provides no floor plans for the fourth story, this upper chamber floor will probably be divided into as many small rooms as possible to accommodate household servants and perhaps an overflow of family children. Here we may also find a ladder or steep stairway leading to the attic space beneath the pitched roof. Dark and airless, this area serves some storage or insulating function. However, it represents possible livable space that future generations may choose to utilize. A simple dormer window would render it minimally hospitable, and, looking farther to the future, a shed dormer or a mansard roof could realize its full potential.

Such tampering with the roofline will be just one of many alterations our house may suffer. It will be piped and plumbed and wired. Its rooms will be subdivided and rearranged and its facade adorned with brackets, bays, and other baubles having little to do with its architectural heritage.

If the house is lucky, it will survive. In this neighborhood, many do. Well built, structurally interdependent, and ultimately adaptable, these houses were designed without a strong definition of function. When adapted to modern living, they can be lived in on modern terms.

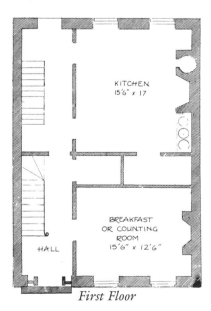

First Floor

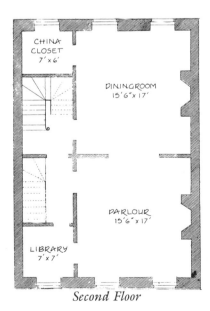

Second Floor

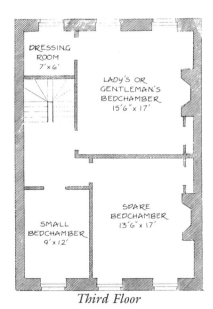

Third Floor

THE SURVIVORS
Early Frame Houses

SOME OF THE OLDEST and most interesting buildings on Beacon Hill have nothing to do with the Mount Vernon Proprietors or trends in early nineteenth-century real estate development. They are tied to the previous century, when a scattering of small wooden houses dotted the acres once occupied by orchards and pastures. By 1814, hundreds of simple frame houses crowded the northern slope of Beacon Hill (see page 19). Freestanding or attached, the house often faced a side yard with its narrow end fronting the street.

These were often the homes of working-class people, and in comparison to their South Slope neighbors they were not always well treated. Freely adapted to the changing times, they served as single house, double house, boarding house, or commercial establishment, according to the practical demands of the day. In consequence, much of the original fabric of these houses has disappeared. What remains is an occasional stairway or mantelpiece, a built-in cupboard or some well-worn old floorboards. To this day, however, their rooms reflect a pleasant, domestic scale and an ambience that is reminiscent of an earlier time. There are about a dozen of these old houses, scattered from Pinckney Street northward with an important cluster on Smith Court. That they have survived at all is in many ways remarkable, and today they are much prized.

This small but well-proportioned room, with its Federal
mantel and finely detailed crown molding, freely
combines objects from different periods — the Empire
mirror, Victorian chairs, modern piano, and fine old
Canton porcelain in the open china closet. The result is
a warm and welcoming room with a distinct but
unpretentious charm.

Historically, one of the most interesting parts of this Pinckney Street house is the old kitchen. The fireplace is original; it is believed to date from the 1790s. When the house was renovated around 1980, the bricks were exposed and the fireplace was fitted with a wood stove. The hearth was laid with modern tiles and the space-saving circular stairway installed. Other antique features in the room include the massive hand-hewn post in the foreground and the exposed ceiling beams. This space now serves as a small family room adjacent to a modern kitchen.

In an early Joy Street house, some of the old pine has been stripped and bleached. Particularly handsome is the mantelpiece with its restrained dentil treatment, a favored motif of Federal-period cabinetmakers. While amply proportioned, this room is extremely simple, with minimal decorative detail. While many features are probably original, the purple window panes are not; the house is much too old to have had them installed when it was built.

This handsomely restored Pinckney Street house probably dates from around 1800, and its history is typical of many Beacon Hill dwellings. Victorianized in the 1850s, it was later converted to a boarding house, and served as one for almost a century. Restoration, which began around 1960, has incorporated both Federal and Victorian features. Here in the dining room, the rich deep-green walls set off both the marble Victorian mantelpiece and the beautifully preserved carved cornice moldings, original to the house.

Tastefully furnished with American antiques, the ground-floor reception room in a 1799 North Slope house exhibits pleasing proportions even though the space is small — about 11 by 13 feet with ceilings just 7 feet high. The simple wooden mantelpiece is original, while built-in closets on the same wall, installed by the present owners in the 1960s, blend nicely with the older features. The high chest is a Pennsylvania piece dating from circa 1770.

HIGH STYLE
The Spirit of the Mansion-House Era

THE PLAN OF THE Mount Vernon Proprietors for an exclusive quarter of elegant mansion-houses never materialized. Falling victim to economic realities, this scheme was abandoned by 1820. Nevertheless, many grand houses continued to be built on the South Slope of Beacon Hill, and many have survived, with varying degrees of integrity.

These houses were custom built on the grand scale, with spacious rooms befitting a prosperous lifestyle. Interior designs were based upon well-established rules of proportion, giving careful attention to decorative details. This was a sophisticated, urban style, in the tradition of English Neo-Classicism. On Beacon Hill, the period achieved a happy blend of elegance with domesticity and comfort.

Attached or freestanding, about thirty such buildings survive on the South Slope of Beacon Hill. Some of them, proving too large for single-family occupancy, have been converted to commercial or institutional use, while others have been divided into smaller residential units. Even the remaining single-family houses have seen extensive alterations, either through modernizations, especially in the Victorian era, or through overzealous restoration. Nevertheless, they stand today, survivors themselves of the Proprietors' vision.

Here is a Mount Vernon Street parlor with the finest Beacon Hill credentials: built by Charles Bulfinch in 1806 and renovated by Ogden Codman in 1891. Now headquarters for the Colonial Society of Massachusetts, it is furnished with pieces presented to the society by members and friends. The mirrors on either side of the mantel came from a Back Bay mansion. This interior was not always so dazzling, however. A photo on page 115 shows a rather more somber view of the same room.

Impeccably restored by the Society for the Preservation of New England Antiquities, the "withdrawing room" of the first Harrison Gray Otis house (page 71) perfectly defines the mansion-house era. The mirror-paneled mahogany doors reflect light from the candle-lit chandelier and girandole over the mantel. The English japanned fancy chairs and porcelain tea set belonged to the Otis family, while musical instruments speak to Mr. Otis's composing talent.

To the left is just a glimpse of a Bulfinch dining room. The intricate tiling on the hearth is a copy of a classical Roman mosaic. The French clock and the large mirror over the mantel are typical of the period. The mirror is positioned to reflect and maximize the light from the cut-glass chandelier, which along with candelabra and girandoles provides the only lighting for this large and gracious room.

The Bulfinch parlor seen at right has been successfully adapted to modern family use. Large overstuffed sofas suit the scale of the room, which is an ample 20 by 24 feet. Only the tall-case clock betrays the 12-foot ceiling height. The cornice, the woodwork, and probably the white Italian marble mantel are original. The gas chandelier has never been electrified.

Like the front door, the entrance hall set the style for the house, and its decorative elements were intended to make a favorable first impression. This spacious entry hall from an 1802 mansion-house features a grand staircase with Georgian-style turned balusters and mahogany handrail. While this part of the house has been considerably altered, the shell pattern of the plaster cornice moldings is original.

Gracefully curving stairs are the focal point in the hall of this 1820 Beacon Street residence. The plain balusters are typical of the later date. Near the head of the stairs is the classically-inspired niche that was a common feature in the stair halls of Beacon Hill houses of various sizes and periods. There is a second, narrower staircase in the back of the house for the use of servants. The parquet floor is modern and faux-painted.

PERIOD PERFECT
Noted Restorations

THE AVERAGE BEACON HILL house has served successive generations of residents for 150 years or more, and each generation has brought some part of the house up to date. Thus, the concept of an historically pure house is theoretical at best, and the chances of finding an historically well-preserved house are slight.

The rooms presented on the following pages are remarkably pure. Most typically, they are the product of either good fortune or extreme neglect. For example, the 1837 Greek Revival house on page 86 has been owned by only three families, all of whom treated it well. For the present owners, who bought the house in 1978, the principal chore was eliminating the Victorian features that had compromised its fine classical details. In contrast, the Victorian dwelling on page 87 had for decades served as a rooming house. Purchased by its present owners in the early 1960s, it was derelict but its details had been left intact.

In both cases, renovation has been a labor of love. From hardware to woodwork to window treatment, all has been meticulously restored. Moreover, structural work was only the beginning. In an ongoing effort, the owners have gradually acquired period furnishings to further complement these carefully appointed rooms.

A small first-floor reception room has been furnished to fit the period
of this 1831 West Cedar Street house. The rich window hangings, the
mirrors above the mantel and at the window pier, the classic ruby-red
damask — all these details are as historically appropriate as the
antiques that furnish the room. The windows face directly onto the
sidewalk, so the interior shutters provide privacy. Divided horizon-
tally, they can be half-closed to allow some daylight to enter the room.

The photos on this page provide two views from the first floor of an 1837 Mount Vernon Street residence. Its Greek Revival credentials are evident in every detail. Above is the dining room, with a symmetrical end wall featuring china cupboards. All the woodwork is original, and the hanging chandelier came with the house. Through the center door is the front reception room, with boldly patterned wall-to-wall carpeting typical of the period. Applied pilasters flank the shuttered windows, between which stands an American Empire side table from the 1830s. The pilasters are used again on a side wall, seen below. Here they set off a mahogany door, which is surmounted by a carved pediment. Framed architectural prints on either side of the door re-state the theme of high classicism.

About forty years separate the chaste reserve on the opposite page from the full-blown Victorian exuberance seen here. Both these views are from a Hancock Street house of the mid-1870s, which has been meticulously restored and interestingly embellished with American Empire pieces. The library, above, is painted in rich, vibrant hues. Paintings hang from silk cords, and every object evokes the period. This room perfectly reflects the Victorian passion for richness and intensity of color and form. Down to the last tassel, it has been thoughtfully and lovingly restored. On the right, a curtained alcove creates a picturesque niche that also serves as a passage-way connecting rooms on either side of the hall. Heavy, dark woodwork produces the somber, cloistered atmosphere that typifies the period.

The front parlor of King's Chapel House, 64 Beacon
Street, contains a beautifully preserved display of
French scenic wallpaper. First printed in 1849 by the
Zuber Company, the pattern, known as "El Dorado,"
has been declared a technical tour-de-force. Printed
in 192 colors from more than 1500 woodblocks, it
depicts extravagantly exotic scenes with admirable
botanic accuracy.

While more modest dwellings of the 1820s and 1830s
usually had no room devoted exclusively to dining, this
house was large enough and grand enough to have one.
The room seen here is in the city-owned Parkman House
(page 29), an 1825 Beacon Street mansion bequeathed
to the city in 1908. Used for decades for municipal
offices, the building was restored in 1974. This view
through double sliding doors reveals an opulence seldom
seen on Beacon Hill: richly carved cornices, Corinthian
columns framing the doors, and an exquisite white
marble mantelpiece of classical refinement. The house
has been furnished with period pieces donated by generous citizens or on loan from the Museum of Fine Arts.

The spacious parlor in an 1849 Temple Street house runs the entire depth of the building. This unusually large room was possible because the house featured an early, limited heating system, which delivered hot air to this floor via a duct into one of the fireplaces. The twin black mantelpieces are original, as are the woodwork and the ceiling moldings with the band of gilded trim. The elaborate mirrors are said to have been moved from a house on Louisburg Square. The present owners are the third family to occupy this house. They use the back half of the room as a dining area and the front half as a parlor. The furnishings are a pleasant mix of comfortable modern pieces and Victorian-period antiques, and a large and varied collection of nineteenth-century Japanese art.

This majestic sweep of stairs makes a strong impression on anyone entering the house. The double newel is unusual on Beacon Hill. The raised platform on each side of the stairs runs the length of the house, providing headroom for a tunnel that passes beneath the building to a service yard in the rear.

EXTRAORDINARY ROOMS
Stunning Re-creations

THE FIVE ROOMS presented on these pages go beyond restoration. Rather, they are creative embellishments that, although not original, respect the history of a house and complement its basic architectural style. The process may involve recycling of architectural materials from other buildings, as was the case with the library on page 93. Sometimes just an idea is recycled, as with the orangery on the same page.

Re-creating a room is a risky undertaking, however, and very often the result is less than convincing. The key to success is a combination of high-quality materials and expert workmanship, plus a generous fund of historical knowledge, good taste, and common sense. Effective decorating and furnishing is probably more important in a reconstructed room than in an original.

If successful, the new room becomes an integral part of the house. Such rooms wear well, and they seem quickly to acquire an inviting, lived-in look . Each of the ones shown here has acquired a patina of character and a sense of respectability in its own right.

This superb room is the original kitchen in an 1827 West Cedar Street house. Built into the slope, the basement level opens onto the garden in the rear. Major renovations in the early 1950s combined new and old elements to transform this area into an atmospheric "tavern room," with exposed bricks and beams, tall leaded-glass windows, and a fireplace wall with bake ovens and an open hearth. The room is finely appointed, with old books, old pewter, and old wood combining to create a mood of romantic nostalgia.

Rich cherry paneling installed in the 1950s introduces a hint of modernism to an 1808 Pinckney Street kitchen, while the raised-hearth fireplace, exposed beams, and hanging copper utensils recall an earlier time. The family dining area in the foreground is just a few steps from the door to a walled garden. The formal dining room on the floor above was once served by a dumbwaiter — a commom feature in Beacon Hill houses, where formal rooms were intentionally distanced from the hubbub of the kitchen.

Measuring 14 by 54 feet, this richly paneled Chestnut Street library is one of the largest rooms on Beacon Hill. Seen here is a view toward the back wall of the room, a 1906 addition to an 1824 house. The abstract painting above the fireplace is an effective focal point; except for this touch, the treatment is traditional. The furniture is arranged in small and comfortable groupings, creating a sense of intimacy despite the generous proportions of the room, which is large enough to accommodate a crowd. Originally used as a ballroom, its paneled walls conceal a secret staircase.

A Victorian-era addition to a Greek Revival Mount Vernon Street dwelling, this library features architectural elements recycled in the 1870s from an unknown English manor. With an eclectic mix of comfortable furniture and family memorabilia, it is a highly personal room, reflecting the owners' lifestyle, whims, and tastes.

A recent addition to a large Beacon Street house, this conservatory provides a breakfast room adjacent to the kitchen and overlooking the newly landscaped garden. Based on the traditional English orangery, this gracious extra room adds a touch of elegance to both house and garden. While conservatories were not original features of Beacon Hill houses, they were being added to London town houses of the same era.

AT HOME
Life in a Beacon Hill Town House

MOST BEACON HILL HOUSES are neither mansion-houses nor "survivors," nor are they particularly remarkable for architectural purity or exquisite detail. Spanning the years between 1820 and the 1840s, they range in style from late Federal to early Victorian, but they are predominantly Greek Revival in character.

The average Beacon Hill dwelling was neither custom built nor designed by an architect. Rather, it was erected on speculation by a housewright, working from a pattern book such as Asher Benjamin's *American Builder's Companion*. This was an era of rapid technical advances, and with each decade builders had access to ever-greater supplies of mass-produced, machine-made materials. Yet, coming from a tradition of classicism, the housewrights tended to pay close attention to the rules of proportion. Moreover, the quality of both materials and workmanship was generally high.

Each of the houses pictured here has its own unique history of ownership. A fortunate few have belonged to only a few loving families, while others have been brutally converted to multi-unit dwellings or commercial use. Some were heavily Victorianized, while others were subjected to excessive modern renovations, but almost every house in the Historic District possesses at least some original detail, plus comfortable proportions and a flexible, livable floor plan that allows the owner great flexibility in lifestyle and decor.

Open and airy, this double drawing room displays the strong architectural character typical of the Greek Revival period. The matching black mantelpieces are very commonly seen in houses of the 1830s, as are the large sliding pocket doors, which allow the space to be used as one room or two. Here on Louisburg Square, these doors are mahogany. The swelling front of the facade is defined by a wallpaper border of classical swags.

The photos on this page, featuring two rooms in an 1826 Mount Vernon Street dwelling, illustrate how flexible an old town house can be. The garden-level room seen above has been converted into a playroom for visiting grandchildren — with toys from previous generations brought forth for the occasion. Although the room has been greatly altered, its location suggests that this was the original kitchen for the house. However, the present owners have moved their kitchen and dining facilities to the third floor, into an area that was probably designed as bedchambers. Seen below, the front chamber adapts perfectly to use as a dining room. Its more modest proportions and simpler details are typical of the bedroom floors, though this house is large enough that even the smaller rooms are ample.

The two bedrooms pictured here reveal the simpler treatment given to upper, non-public parts of the house, with lower ceilings, shorter windows, and little decorative detail. The room seen above features an antique four-poster with toile hangings that match the window curtains. The bed is a family piece whose owner is, in fact, a desendent of a Mount Vernon Proprietor. The slant-top desk dates from around 1810. The third-floor guest room below is appointed as a pleasant sitting room when not in use. Richly decorated with coordinated wallpaper and fabric, it is furnished with a pair of nineteenth-century French sleigh beds and other antique pieces, including the bed stairs.

Whatever the age of a house, an efficient, up-to-date kitchen is essential. The second-floor room pictured above was once a library. The present owners of this North Slope house chose it as the kitchen because it is bright and sunny with access to the roof deck. The remodeled room retains its original door frames and cornice moldings, and the painted cabinets were custom built in a compatible design with a combination of solid and glass doors. The kitchen appliances and fixtures are in a low-key modern style that blends with the room's traditional look. A slipcovered wing chair next to the breakfast table offers a comfortable seat.

When new owners bought an 1824 Chestnut Street house (top opposite), they acquired an old cooking range along with an out-of-date kitchen. Thus, they were immediately faced with the question of whether to remove the range or plan a new kitchen around it. Choosing the second option, they not only saved the stove but made it the focal point of the room. The color scheme is dramatic, with a traditional black-and-white tile floor and bright yellow walls that enhance an already sunny room. The panel above the range is a section of an eighteenth-century French mural, found in a shop on Charles Street. The owners' collection of majolica adds another personal touch.

In another recent renovation, the owners of a large Mount Vernon Street residence have dramatically changed some of the interior spaces of their house while retaining its most striking architectural details. Furnished in a contemporary mode, the bowed front parlor (below) respects the scale and symmetry of the original room. Tall south-facing windows admit ample light, enhancing a color scheme that combines warm and cool pastels. The kitchen (above) occupies the long wall of the original stair hall. The bracketed stone pediment over the stovetop is an element from a sixteenth-century mantel, removed from the mansion at 107 Chestnut Street (page 65) and discovered by the owners of this house in a salvage shop. Installing the pediment in the kitchen, they used the verticals to create the pier table seen between the living room windows.

No wonder this Chestnut Street parlor exhibits an air of character and style. This house, built in 1823, has been owned by the same Beacon Hill family for almost sixty years. With a highly personal collection of family portraits and memorabilia, it overlooks one of the loveliest gardens on Beacon Hill. The shimmering silver paper on the walls is a reminder of earlier days. Inspired by the sheets that once lined tea chests arriving from the Orient, it became a favorite wall covering in many Boston and Salem homes.

Furnished for comfort, a second-floor library on West Cedar Street provides a cozy retreat for reading or conversation. The English fruitwood paneling was installed in the early 1900s. The room contains numerous mementos of the owners' travels. The lamps near the fireplace are crafted from brass Venetian horses, and the mantel shelf displays a collection of Chinese ivory carvings.

Almost every Beacon Hill house retains some vestiges of its early years, before the development of modern domestic technologies. The pictures on this page present a sampling of such reminders: a unique gas fixture (right); an original example of the Rumford Roaster, an early improvement in cooking technology, which survives in the old kitchen at 40 Beacon Street; and two early bathrooms, added to houses around the turn of the century.

CONVERSIONS
Recycled for Modern Living

PUTTING OLD BUILDINGS to new use is not a modern idea. One of the earliest conversions on Beacon Hill was probably that of 24 Pinckney Street (page 50), the 1802 stable that served as a grocery in the 1830s and was fancifully remodeled as a residence fifty years later.

Since the 1950s, two forces have combined to stimulate conversion of existing structures. First, the creation of the Beacon Hill Historic District essentially froze the exterior aspect of Beacon Hill streets; since that time, except for a very few destroyed by fire, not a single building has been lost. In addition, ever-rising property values have encouraged the development of every square foot of potentially usable space.

By far the greatest number of recycled buildings are the old stables, a leftover commodity of Beacon Hill's horse-and-carriage years. Dozens of these structures are now comfortable dwellings. Other major conversions have involved the refurbishing of large institutional structures, such as the Boston University School of Theology to apartments in 1965; the Bowdoin School to elderly housing in 1977; the Charles Street Meeting House to shops and offices in 1982; and the old English High School building to condominiums in 1984.

Adapting old buildings to new uses can involve considerable restructuring or total gutting. The resulting spaces can be very theatrical, and architectural treatments range from traditional to ultramodern, offering a rare opportunity here on Beacon Hill to create a highly personal environment.

Conversion of an old school building resulted in rooms of dramatic proportions, such as this living room with its great arched windows and 16-foot ceilings. The new owners admit that furnishing this room was initially a challenge. Their solution was both simple and practical: to re-use much of the furniture they already owned, a pleasant combination of antique and modern pieces, and allow the soaring dimensions of the room to make a separate architectural statement.

This living room, for all its old-world charm, was created from scratch. In a 1968 conversion, a large carriage house was completely gutted and its interior rebuilt as a comfortable modern home. The mantelpiece is an antique that the owner reclaimed from a Back Bay house. The room is personalized by collections of various objets-d'art, and the traditional furniture grouping in front of the fire creates an intimate setting.

This former stable on Byron Street was also totally rebuilt. The conversion, accomplished in 1970, arranged the living quarters around an atrium, which is the only light source for many of the rooms in this house. The glass walls that surround the atrium on three sides bring this courtyard, with its seasonal interest, indoors. The espaliered yew on the brick wall has thrived in this environment for more than twenty years.

In another view of the carriage house seen opposite, the space has been dramatically arranged to create a two-story entrance hall. Lit by a skylight, it has been decoratively paved with brick, slate, and marble. Against a surviving section of old brick wall and supplemented by artificial light, the owner maintains a small but exotic indoor garden. From the balcony hang a seventeenth-century tapestry and a clerical cope dating from the 1800s.

A converted tenement on Phillips Street has been divided into an owner-occupied triplex and a duplex apartment above. Seen here is the living room of the triplex, which is entered from the front hall but is internally connected to the ground-level kitchen via the old cellar stairs and to the upper bedroom floor by a modern spiral unit. These buildings are well built and structurally flexible; this is the third North Slope tenement these owners have converted.

GREENINGS
Horticulture on the Hill

EXCEPT FOR THE freestanding mansion-houses, few Beacon Hill dwellings were built with gardens. Land was scarce, and the yards behind the row houses were given to the functional activities of the household. Not until the advent of modern plumbing, kitchen, and laundry facilities did these spaces become available for more amenable purposes. In 1929, a group of neighbors joined to form the Beacon Hill Garden Club, whose annual tour of the Hidden Gardens of Beacon Hill attracts several thousand visitors each May.

There are hundreds of walled gardens on Beacon Hill today. Within these very restricted areas, homeowners have created secluded, highly personal retreats that are so intimately related to the house that they are often considered as extra, outdoor rooms. Used for cookouts, dining, or alfresco entertaining, the garden can also function as a play yard, a dog run, or a place to park the family car.

Not all gardening is done at ground level. A view from above reveals hundreds of roofdecks not visible from the street. As gardens, patios, or sundecks, most accessible rooftops have been appropriated for some use.

Green thumbs are also exercised at streetside, with large front lawns on Mount Vernon Street, pocket gardens on Chestnut, and in other locations just treepits. Since 1958, an annual competition has encouraged window-box gardeners, whose efforts are so prolific that, along with the gaslight, the window box has become a symbol of Beacon Hill.

BEACON HILL ALBUM
Portraits of a Neighborhood, Today and Yesterday

ON THIS SITE
STOOD THE HOME OF
JOHN SINGLETON COPLEY
DISTINGUISHED HISTORICAL AND
PORTRAIT PAINTER
BORN IN BOSTON IN 1737
DIED IN LONDON IN 1815
PLACED BY THE CITY OF BOSTON 1925

THIS TABLET RESTORED BY
THE GEORGE B HENDERSON FOUNDATION

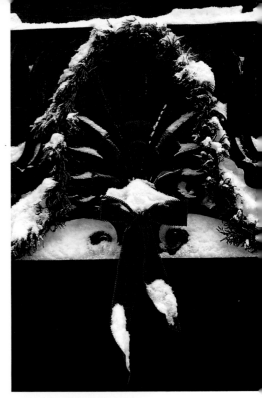

Early views of Beacon Hill: Clockwise from right: Numbers 1 and 2 Otis Place, circa 1880; Chestnut Street, looking west toward Charles, before 1916; the Boston skyline as seen from the West Boston Bridge, 1864; the Amory-Ticknor house, still standing at the Beacon-Park corner, circa 1870.

Lost views: Clockwise from above: Northwest corner of
Joy and Myrtle streets (site of Beacon Chambers), 1870;
Pemberton Square, circa 1880; the Francis B. Winter
House, northwest corner of Myrtle and Anderson
streets, demolished 1905; 97 Mount Vernon Street
(corner of West Cedar), before 1870.

People and places: Clockwise from above: 85 Mount Vernon (the Second Otis House), date unknown; 141 Cambridge Street (the First Otis House) before restoration, 1916; "Battle of the Bricks," West Cedar Street, 1947; the Swan Stables, 50-60 Mount Vernon Street, 1907.

Interior views: Clockwise from above: front hall, the Gardner Brewer house, 29 Beacon Street, circa 1880; parlor, 87 Mount Vernon Street, circa 1901; parlor, the Tudor house, 34 Beacon Street, circa 1880; library, Governor Andrew house, 110 Charles Street, circa 1865; parlor, 37 1/2 Beacon Street (date unknown).

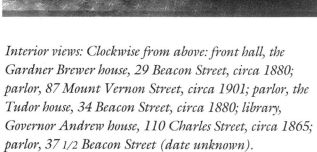

MODEL HOMES
An Architectural Guide to Beacon Hill Houses

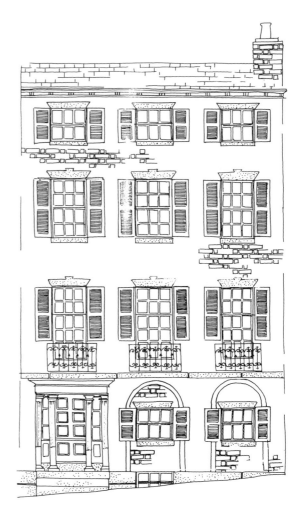

THE HOUSES SEEN on these pages cannot be found on any Beacon Hill street. Rather, they are prototypes — composite drawings that present the stylistic evolution of the Beacon Hill town house from its Federal beginnings to its Victorian conclusion. We approach this task with trepidation because we are delving into a field crowded with both aficionados and experts. Thus we hastily offer the following caveat: the drawings on these pages are merely fanciful renderings, concocted by us to illustrate the general characteristics of the various architectural periods on Beacon Hill.

The classifications and labels are intended as a basis for looking at individual facades. We hope this section will render a stroll down any Beacon Hill street a more interesting and enriching experience.

Those who use these pages must remember: (1) styles did not change overnight — at any given time both old-fashioned and avant-garde buildings were being erected; (2) the periods so overlap each other that almost no building can be considered pure; and, (3) almost all buildings have seen subsequent alterations either to modernize or to restore them.

In preparing these drawings, we have relied heavily on Carl J. Weinhardt, Jr.'s, "The Domestic Architecture of Beacon Hill, 1800-1850," which appeared in the 1958 *Proceedings* of the Bostonian Society. This detailed discussion is lucid and informative, and the accompanying illustrations by Henry A. Millon were an inspiration for those that follow.

LARGE HOUSE, CIRCA 1805

Bricks: rough and irregular; laid with wide joints in Flemish bond

Cornice: usually wood

Entryway: flat-headed with rectangular lights; portico of wood

Foundation: low, granite

Height: four stories plus attic

Ironwork: delicate wrought iron; individual balconies

String course: between first and second floors

Window lintels: stone, flared, sometimes with keystones

Windows: first floor often set in arched recesses; graduated heights; parlor floor tall and triple hung

SMALL HOUSE, CIRCA 1805

Bricks: rough and irregular; laid with wide joints in Flemish bond

Cornice: usually wood

Entryway: flat-headed with rectangular lights; sometimes recessed

Foundation: very low, granite

Height: four stories plus attic

Ironwork: none

Window lintels: not common

Windows: triple window on ground floor; 6/6 (six panes over six) above; 3/3 on top floor

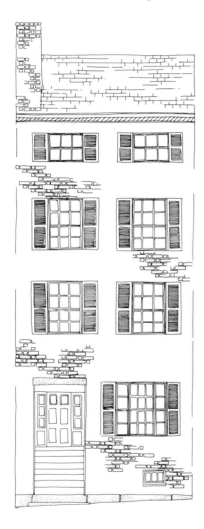

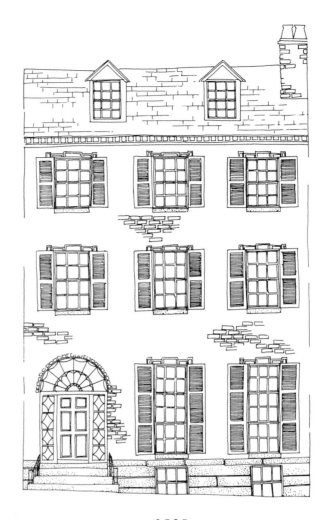

LARGE HOUSE OF THE 1820s

Bricks: smoother and more uniform; laid with narrower joints in English or common bond

Cornice: brick, dentil pattern

Entryway: arched, often recessed; leaded-glass side and fan lights

Foundation: raised granite

Height: three stories plus attic

Ironwork: usually wrought iron; balconies not common

Window lintels: usually rectangular, often incised

Windows: 6/9 on parlor floor, 6/6 elsewhere

FLEMISH BOND: One of the most dependable indicators of Federal-period construction is the presence of bricks laid in Flemish bond — that is, with alternating ends (headers) and sides (stretchers), as illustrated. Almost universal before 1810, the system gradually gave way to simpler bonding patterns and by 1820 had almost disappeared.

SMALL HOUSE OF THE 1820s

Bricks: smoother and more uniform; laid with
  narrower joints in English or common bond
Cornice: brick, dentil pattern
Entryway: arched and recessed; leaded-glass side and
  fan lights
Foundation: raised granite
Height: three stories plus attic
Ironwork: not common
Window lintels: usually rectangular, often incised
Windows: triple window on one or more floors, 6/6
  elsewhere

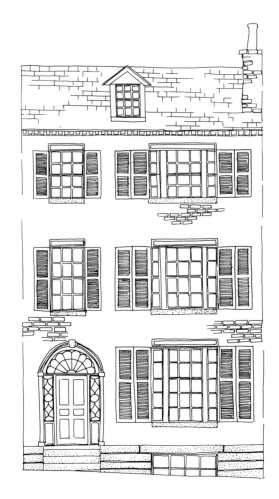

SMALL HOUSE OF THE 1830s

Bricks: smooth and uniform in shape and color; laid
  with tight joints in English or common bond
Cornice: brick, dentil pattern
Entryway: flat-headed; rectangular lights
Foundation: raised granite
Height: three stories plus attic
Ironwork: not common
Window lintels: rectangular, often brownstone
Windows: 6/6

A GREEK REVIVAL HOUSE, VICTORIANIZED
(CIRCA 1870)

Cornice: often trimmed with wood, brick, or brownstone

Entryway: ornate wooden doors, often paired

Foundation: original granite, or replaced with brownstone

Ironwork: heavy cast-iron designs

Roof: frequently mansard

Window lintels: often trimmed with bracketed brownstone

Windows: 2/2; bay windows common

LARGE HOUSE OF THE 1830s

Bricks: smooth and uniform in shape and color; laid with tight joints in English or common bond

Cornice: brick, dentil pattern

Entryway: flat-headed with classical portico in stone; rectangular lights

Foundation: high raised granite

Height: three or four stories plus attic

Ironwork: cast iron, often with classical motifs; continuous balconies

Window lintels: rectangular, often brownstone

Windows: 6/9 on parlor floor, 6/6 elsewhere

ACKNOWLEDGEMENTS

The authors wish to thank the following individuals for neighborly advice, cooperation, and assistance in preparing this book: Robert L. Beal, Emily Belliveau, Sally Brewster, Rick and Nonnie Burnes, Linda Cox, Nathan H. and Denise M. Dewing, Stuart Drake, Alexandra Warburton Eacker, Mr. and Mrs. Edwin I. Firestone, Dr. and Mrs. Frank J. Kefferstan, Mrs. John M. Kingsland, Ariel Lee, Joan and Henry Lee, Mr. and Mrs. Charles N. Leef, Arrel and Robert Linderman, Nancy Macmillan, Kenneth A. MacRae, Jim Mahoney, Frank McGuire, Dr. and Mrs J. Wallace McMeel, Jim McNeely, Susan McW. McNeely, Judith Rice Millon, Richard C. Nylander, William B. Osgood, Robert and Elizabeth Owens, Jeanne Muller Ryan, Sue and Garret Schenck, The Reverend Carl R. Scovel, S. Parkman Shaw, Jane and Tad Stahl, Lise Lange Striar, Dr. William E. Strole, Dan and Karen Taylor, Mr. and Mrs. Thomas H. Townsend, Mr. and Mrs. James D. Wallace, and Mrs. Peter C. Welch.

We also gratefully acknowledge the invaluable assistance of the following: American Meteorological Society, Dan Macmillan and *The Beacon Hill News*, Sally Pierce and the Boston Athenaeum, Philip Bergen and the Bostonian Society, the Colonial Society of Massachusetts, King's Chapel, Chris Steele and the Massachusetts Historical Society, Robert Clark Rogers and the Parkman House (City of Boston), Lorna Conlon and the Society for the Preservation of New England Antiquities.

PHOTO CREDITS

All color photos that appear on these pages are the work of Southie Burgin, with the following exceptions: page 25 — Aerial Photos International, Inc.; page 28, bottom — courtesy Massachusetts State Senate; pages 29 top and bottom right, 33 bottom right, 34, 38 top left, 39 top right, 40, 52, 56, 59 top center, 73 top left, 107 top left and top right, 109 top center and right, and 111 top center — Barbara W. Moore; pages 39 bottom, 43 top left, 48, 69 top, 109 bottom right, and 110 middle row center and right — Gail Weesner; pages 68 bottom left — photo by Don West, courtesy Museum of Afro American History; page 82 top photo by David Bohl, courtesy Society for the Preservation of New England Antiquities; pages 100 top and 101 center — Thomas H. Townsend; page 109 middle row left and 110 top — Thomas E. Weesner; page 111, middle row right — Ginger Lawrence.

Black-and-white photos on pages 112-115 were made available through the courtesy of: Boston Athenaeum (17 lower left, 112 middle row right, 113 bottom left, 114 bottom left, 115 bottom right); Bostonian Society (112 bottom, 113 top left and right and bottom right, 115 middle row right); Massachusetts Historical Society (17 lower right); Society for the Preservation of New England Antiquities (114 top right, 115 top right and bottom left); *The Beacon Hill News* (114 bottom right); Thomas M. Paine (115 top right).